Wood Pellet Smoker and Grill Cookbook

200+ DELICIOUS RECIPES TO SHOW YOUR FAMILY AND FRIENDS YOUR PITMASTER'S GAME

BY **MICHAEL DRIFTWOOD**

CONTENTS

4

CHAPTER 1
Introduction

Wood Pellets

It's often difficult to identify which brand to consider with the hundreds of different varieties and brands of wood pellets. If you're not sure what brand to opt for, it might help try at least three top three brands you know of and compare their efficiency.

APPEARANCE

The first factor to consider when choosing a brand of wood pellets is the appearance of the pellets. After using wood pellets for some time, you will only tell and judge their quality by how they appear. The first thing to check is the length of the pellets. Brands adhere to specific standards, so this isn't a concern. Nevertheless, you need to understand that when it comes to pellet fuels, length matters, as it will affect the performance of the pellets. The dust you will find in the packaging is also another to consider. It's normal to see fines once you open the bag, but if there's an unusual number of fines, it means the pellets aren't of good quality.

TEXTURE

The texture of the pellets is another thing. Wood pellets have a specific texture in them. If you feel that the pellets are smooth and shiny, it means they are of good quality. The same applies if the pellets do not have cracks. If the pellets are too rough with unusual racks on the surface, it means they are bad quality pellets. This is usually a result of incorrect pressing ratio and moisture content of the raw materials used in making the pellets.

Wood pellets are made by exposing them to high temperatures within a sealed space. During the process, the lignin contained in the biomass material is mixed with other elements, producing a smell of burnt fresh wood. If the pellets smell bad, there's a huge chance they haven't been appropriately processed or contain impure, raw material.

Aside from the appearance, texture, and smell of the wood pellets, another way to check their quality is to see how it reacts with water. Put a handful of pellets in a bowl of water, and allow them to settle for several minutes.

If the pellets dissolve in the water and expand quickly, this means they are of good quality. On the other hand, if the pellets don't disappear within minutes but instead expand and become hard, they are of bad quality.

Finally, try burning some of the pellets, as well. If the wood pellets are of excellent quality, the flame they produce will be bright and brown. If the fire they produce is dark in color, it means the pellet's quality is not good. Good-quality pellets also produce a little ash, so if the pellets leave you with a lot of residues, it's a sign that the pellets are bad quality.

If your new smoker grill needs assembly, follow the steps included in the owner's manual. Carefully attach the legs, the grill door, the flue or chimney, and the drip catcher plate. You will want to have the right amount of heavy-duty aluminum foil handy as well. Remember, read the assembly steps carefully before beginning, and don't rush. This is a fun time!

From the hopper, the pellets are fed into a cooking chamber by an electrically powered auger. Then through burning, the wood pellets burst into flames in the cooking area.

Air will be brought in by intake fans. Heat smoke then spread in the cooking area and over steaks, ribs, and burgers.

When your grill is assembled and ready to fire up, have your pellet supply near.
Open the door and remove the grill, put oil in the drain pan, and check heat from inside the grill.

The switch must be in the off position.

- Open the hopper lid and look for the drill.
- Make sure there are no other objects in the auger.
- Switch on the temperature to smoke, and then look in the hopper to see if the drill is working.
- Fill the hopper with your choice of pellets.
- Do not use heating fuel pellets in the grill and turn the temperature to a high program.
- In the first charging of the auger, the pellets will take time to travel from the pellet hopper to the fire pot.
- Once the pellets start to fall into the fire pot, switch the temperature to the shutdown.
- Set the temperature to smoke and let the pellets into a full fire. When the flames come out of the fire pot, turn the temperature to shut down, and let it cool.
- To clean easily, put heavy-duty aluminum foil in the drain grease pan. Make sure the edges and ends of the foil are tight against the bottom of the drain.
- With the door open, set the temperature to smoke program.
- You will see whitish-gray smoke coming out of the grill as the pellets ignite after two minutes.
- When the pellets catch fire, close the door and set the temperature to any cooking setting you want.
- Season the first batch of food before cooking. Close the door for forty-five minutes and turn the temperature to high.
- Before putting food on the grill, preheat the grill for ten minutes while the door closed.
- Start your grill on the smoke setting only.

For your first time out, remember that you have a great device that features the most excellent characteristics for great results. Just set the temperature control, and add the correct number of pellets, and the smoker will take it from there. This is a designed cooker that is very easy to use.

The Pallet Smoker Grill is a versatile grill that outcooks any other type of outdoor grill bar. Set the "low & slow" for long, slow meat searing, and when you are ready, with a comprehensive understanding of the new grill, use the more complicated recipes.

Hardwood pellets and flavored pellets provide something special to your food. This gives it the excellent smoke flavor, and long, all-day smoked meats are something to experience, thanks to the "set and forget" setting that takes care of the temperature. With this, you automatically add your fuel pellets.

CHAPTER 2

Smoker & Grill Basics

How to Choose Your Meat

From meat selection to the proper resting time, the full smoking process must take seriously to have the highest quality results. Every part of the process can affect your results—making the difference between the burnt and blue-ribbon quality.

📖 PORK

Pork has a salty flavor that cannot be mistaken. The fat content in pork, though it can get in the way at times, allows it to be both juicy and tender. Pork goes extremely well with sweet flavors, and I refer to that a lot. Pick up some local honey; it supports the beekeepers, farmers, and markets in the area. Plus, local honey tastes better. Brown sugar is delicious with pork, too.

📖 PORK RIBS

When dealing with pork ribs, both spareribs and baby backs. you want to select a cut with a good amount of fat, but it should be consistent throughout. Too much fat, especially if it is only in certain places, can make for an unappetizingly fatty bite.

- Remove the membrane.
- Use mustard as a binder.
- Use whatever liquid you like best (including beer or wine, but not liquor) for spritz or your wrap.
- Country-style ribs are ribs. Cook boneless country-style ribs the same way you would other ribs. The smoked flavor is great, and they are extremely tender when done.

📖 PORK SHOULDER

When selecting your pork shoulder, it doesn't matter if you choose one with or without a bone. Do check the fat content. You want some fat, or your pork will dry out, but too much can be overly fatty, just like ribs. The fat cap should be less than 1 inch deep.

- Inject your pork shoulder for extra moisture and flavor.
- Smoke your pork longer for a good "bark."
- Use your hands when pulling the meat—it's just easier.

TENDERLOINS

Pork tenderloins are among the simplest smoke preparations on the grill, but they're always impressive. When selecting tenderloins, as with most pork, the key is fat content. Try to limit the fat content on tenderloins. A pellet grill will work to keep them moist and will limit dried-out areas.

- Use a reverse sear.
- Pork tenderloins are a great candidate for marinating.

BEEF

Selecting beef is made easier by its grade.

BRISKET

Brisket tends to be the gold standard, and among the most difficult to cook, on the pellet grill. Many looks at the perfect brisket with reverence and hope for the day when they'll successfully achieve it. When selecting the perfect brisket with both the point and flat cuts, the key is not too much fat.

- Get rid of that fat cap. A huge fat cap is just not appetizing if you leave it on when you smoke your brisket. Use a boning knife or whatever knife you have available and cut the fat cap down to about ¼ inch. Trimming the fat cap will decrease the fattiness of your brisket, but leaving it partially there will keep the meat moist.
- Wrap. Don't wrap. You choose.
- If you don't wrap the meat, spritz it, or use a water pan.

BEEF BACK RIBS

Beef back ribs can be amazing, but they can also be a lot of work. Make sure you select meaty beef ribs. Many beef ribs are cut far too close to the bone, leaving little meat, only what exists between the bones.

- Try them dry rubbed.
- Use Worcestershire sauce for spritz for extra flavor.
- Peppered ribs are fantastic. Black pepper is great with beef. Use freshly ground black pepper on your beef ribs for amazing flavor.

📖 POULTRY

Poultry is a central part of our food culture and history. From the Thanksgiving turkey to chicken noodle soup for the common cold, poultry is everywhere.

📖 WHOLE CHICKEN

Cooking chicken is an excellent way to learn to use a pellet grill. A whole chicken can be smoked before roasting as well, giving it extra flavor.
- *Rub your chicken with oil as well as seasoning.*
- *Injecting a whole chicken with liquid can change it from a pedestrian to something that can only be described as amazing.*
- *When you rub your chicken, get the rub between the skin and the breast meat.*

📖 CHICKEN WINGS

Wings cooked on a pellet grill or smoker are perfect for one reason: smoke.
- *If you don't already have some favorite sauces, learn to make some or get some. Wings are good dry, but they're better with sauce.*
- *This is another instance where cast iron is good. Use a small cast-iron pot to keep your sauce warm. This is also where you can mix things up.*
- *Try making sweet-and-sour wings. Use an Asian- or Thai-style rub for the wings. Once they reach an internal temperature of 165°F to 170°F, coat them in a sweet-and-sour sauce and finish for 10 minutes more at 300°F.*
- *Experiment with dry rubs.*

📖 TURKEY

The pellet grill or smoker is perfect for making that smoky yet moist golden bird. When selecting turkey, don't get one that is already brined. You will make it extra salty by doing it again or injecting it.
- *Baste your turkey with butter. This is certainly not the healthiest way of cooking it, but it is the tastiest.*
- *Use your thermometer.*
- *Don't put a stuffed turkey on the grill.*

📖 TURKEY DRUMSTICKS

In selecting a turkey drumstick, always remember that bigger is better.

- *Just like with whole chicken, rub some seasoning under the skin. Rubbing seasoning under the skin allows the meat to take on the flavor better.*
- *For turkey legs, go a little higher on your cooking temperature (400°F+).*
- *All poultry can be cooked similarly. Cooking suggestions in the poultry units apply to both chicken and turkey. The flavors and cooking styles are similar.*

📖 LAMB CHOPS

- *You can use rib chops, as they are the most tender, but loin or shoulder chops are great, and shoulder chops are so tasty.*
- *Lamb chops are perfect with a reverse sear.*
- *Mince your herbs for lamb chops and rub them into your meat.*
- *Go slightly overboard on the black pepper. The pepper gives your lamb a little kick.*

📖 LEG OF LAMB

A leg of lamb can be roasted, smoky perfection. The wood-fired flame gives it that old-world taste and packs it with moist flavor.

When selecting your leg, try not to go too lean. The fat in the leg, like most other meats, will work to keep the meat from drying out while roasting. Bone-in or out is a preference. Although bone-in may give slightly more flavor, it is more difficult to cut.

- *Smoke lamb leg before roasting. Smoking the leg will allow it to absorb more smoke flavor. Give it at least 1 hour to smoke.*
- *Cook lamb over an open flame.*
- *Garlic also complements lamb well.*

📖 SALMON

When selecting salmon, always choose wild over farmed for better flavor and because it's typically fresh, not frozen.

- *Use a cedar plank for smoking and barbecuing salmon.*
- *If you do grill salmon directly on the grate, oil the grates beforehand.*
- *Hit the meat of the fish with an open flame after smoking.*
- *Use mayonnaise or Dijon mustard to keep salmon moist. Applying*

a thin coat of mayonnaise or mustard to your salmon before cooking it will keep the fish from drying out.

TUNA

Tuna is like most seafood. Try for fresh, if you can. Avoid anything that looks dried out or like it may have freezer burn.
· Try a reverse sear on tuna for a slight smoke flavor.
· Dill is amazing on tuna like it is on most seafood.
· I use dill weed a lot on seafood, but it is best on tuna steaks. Sprinkle on a generous amount for great flavor.
· Be careful not to overcook the fish.

SHRIMP

From blackened to barbecued, there are many spectacular ways of preparing shrimp, and the pellet grill only adds to the variety. Try to find fresh, never-frozen shrimp and always choose full-size shrimp, not the little salad.
· Best shrimp is the Cajun or Creole Louisiana-style shrimp, but there are all kinds of ways to prepare shrimp on your pellet grill.
· Lemon is an excellent complement to shrimp. Use it in the cooking or after for squeezing.
· Grill baskets are worth their price and great for cooking shrimp.

OYSTERS

In the shell is how we will usually prepare oysters on the pellet grill or smoker. Aim for medium size because they're easy to deal with and eat.
· Peek at your oysters often, but quickly. Drying out the oysters is what you want to avoid, so you must keep tabs on them carefully, but the lid needs to be closed to cook them.

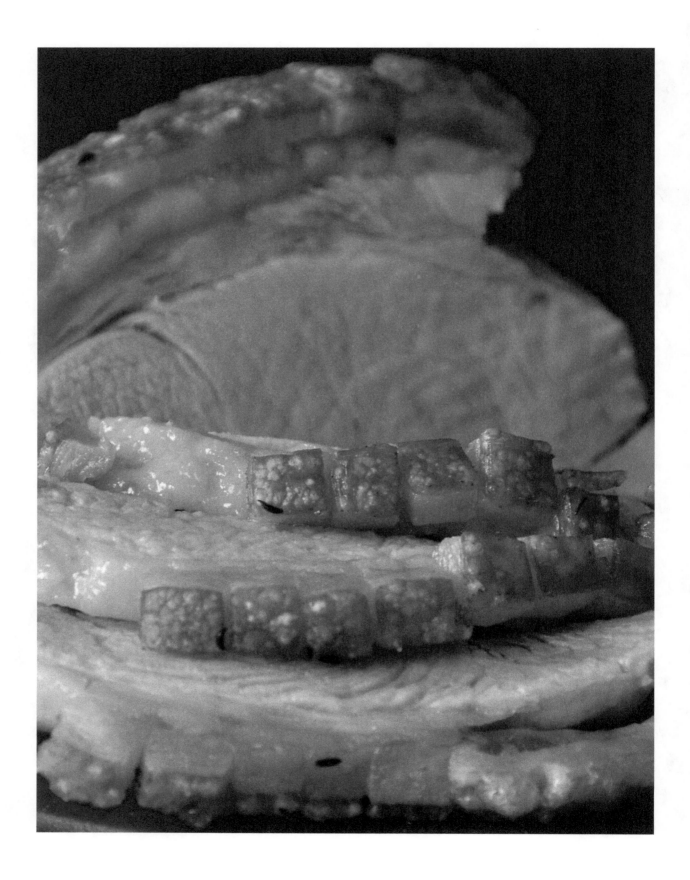

Smoking Times and Temperatures

The first step towards becoming a pit master is to know the exact temperatures to smoke your food at and the time to pull it out of the cooker. However, one thing you need to know is that even experts are guided by a digital meat thermometer. As such, you need to invest in a good digital thermometer, as it will help measure the internal temperature of the food and the smoker.

BEEF SMOKING TIME & TEMPERATURES

Time	Smoking Temp	Finished Temp
Back ribs	3 – 4 hr	225 – 250 °F
Brisket	12 – 20 hr	225 – 250 °F
Short ribs	6 – 8 hr	225 – 250 °F
Prime rib (4 lbs)	1 hr	225 – 250 °F
Tenderloin	2.5 – 3 hr	225 – 250 °F

PORK SMOKING TIMES & TEMPERATURES

Time	Smoking Temp	Finished Temp
Baby back ribs	5 hr	225 – 250 °F
Belly bacon	6 hr	< 100 °F
Whole pork	16 -18 hr	225 – 250 °F
Sausage	1 – 3 hr	225 – 250 °F
Baby back ribs	2.5 – 3 hr	225 – 250 °F
Baby back ribs	5 hr	225 – 250 °F

POULTRY SMOKING TIMES & TEMPERATURES

Time	Smoking Temp	Finished Temp
Whole chicken	2 – 3 hr	275 – 350 °F
Chicken thighs	1.5 hr	275 – 350 °F
Chicken wings	1.25 hr	275 – 350 °F
Whole turkey	4 – 5 hr	275 – 350 °F
Turkey leg	2 – 3 hr	275 – 350 °F
Turkey wings	2 – 2.5 hr	275 – 350 °F
Turkey breast	4 hr	275 – 350 °F
QUAIL /PHEASANT	1 hr	225 °F
WHOLE DUCK	4 hr	225 – 250 °F

VEGETABLES SMOKING TIMES & TEMPERATURES

Time	Smoking Temp	Finished Temp
Smoked Corn	1.5 – 2 hr	225 – 240 °F
Smoked Potatoes	2 - 3 hr	225 – 240 °F
Boudin	2 hr	225 – 240 °F
Brats	2 hr	225 – 240 °F

Remember, these smoking and finished cooking temperatures are just here to guide you. There are many other factors that can affect your doneness level, or lack of it, including:
·   Meat thickness
·   Fat content of the meat
·   Weather
·   The insulation of your cooker
·   And many others.

ALL ABOUT WOOD SMOKE

Will it smoke? Due to mankind's long history of cooking over live fire, there are unlimited combinations of animal, vegetable, and hardwood smoke flavor.

Remember: Wood pellet grills should only be fueled by food-safe pellets. With wood pellets, you can mix and match your smoke profile to achieve unique flavors—something you cannot do easily with other smokers. The pellets are also easy to store and move, due to their compact nature. However, note that wood pellet grills are limited to pellet fuel that is available commercially, which can be somewhat expensive, hard to find locally, and/or limited in variety. But with blossoming competition, the price, availability, and variety of wood pellets are getting better every year.

WOOD PELLETS 101

Wood pellet grills have become popular because they offer a level of consistency that burning natural logs cannot. Competition cooks love to know that their heat will stay consistent over time and that flavor profiles will remain the same week in and week out. The compressed sawdust is free from impurities, so wood pellets burn cleanly and effectively, maintaining optimal temperature control. Most wood pellet grills consume about a half pound of pellets per hour on a low smoke setting. At higher temperatures, near 450°F, you'll burn about 2.3 pounds per hour. Wind, weather conditions, and cold meat in the cook chamber will also affect burn rate.

One of the joys of wood pellet grills is finding the perfect hardwood for your recipe. Consider your locale: Texas cooks use a lot of native mesquite and oak. I live in South Carolina, so pecan is indigenous and popular. Finally, competition cooks like to get elaborate, combining blends of different woods or even cooking with layers of wood flavor at different points in the cook. Feel free to experiment.

FOOD-GRADE WOOD PELLETS

I've searched high and low for online and local sources of wood pellets, looking for the best price. Again, the big issue is that you need to use food-grade pellets. I've been able to find 100 percent oak pellets at tempting prices; however, there is still no guarantee that impure and potentially toxic wood finishes, varnish, or worse haven't been mixed into the scrap wood used to make these cheaper versions. That's the importance of the USDA food-grade label.

Many grill manufacturers have also gotten into providing their own brands of hardwood pellets. It's important to note that you don't need to stick with your grill manufacturer's brand of wood pellet. It's good to shop around for pricing.

More and more often, the big box retailers that sell wood pellet grills are also selling pellet fuel. Avoiding shipping costs can help keep your expenses down. Plus, you can occasionally find the best prices locally. The lowest price I've found is $16.88 for a 40-pound sack of food-grade Pit Boss Competition Blend at Lowe's. Online, you can typically find food-grade pellets priced at about $20 for a 20-pound bag. Shipping costs could affect total price, so it would be smart to seek out online retailers that offer free shipping.

When you find a good value on wood pellets, it makes sense to store away a surplus. Not only are pellets food-safe, but there is also no shelf life to worry about. Simply keep them dry and you can store them for years. I also recommend keeping your pellets in rodent-and insect-proof containers.

WOOD FLAVORED PELLETS

Smoke flavor is an element of a recipe that defies other senses. It's a flavor that connects you subconsciously to a primitive smell of a specific time and place. Like revisiting a great song, reexperiencing a smoke-infused bite can take you back to a special time and place in a way that other senses cannot. Building recipes around hardwood flavors is one of the joys of smoking. Have fun experimenting and exploring! The following chart outlines the types of food-grade wood pellets currently available on the market.

SINGLE-FLAVOR FOOD-GRADE WOOD PELLETS

WOOD	FLAVOR	WHAT TO COOK WITH IT
ALDER	Delicate, with a hint of sweetness.	Good for fish, pork, poultry, light meat game birds (such as quail and dove), and especially great with salmon.
APPLE	Slightly sweet, but dense, fruity smoke flavor.	Good for beef, poultry, game birds, pork, and ham.
CHERRY	Slightly sweet, fruity smoke flavor.	Good with all meats.
HICKORY	Pungent, smoky, bacon-like flavor, it's the most common wood used for barbecue.	Good for all smoking, especially pork and ribs; it is the most popular grilling wood in the South.
MAPLE	Mild smoky, somewhat sweet flavor.	Good with pork, poultry, cheese, vegetables, and small game birds.
MESQUITE	Strong, earthy flavor.	Good for most meats—especially beef—and most vegetables; it's the most popular grilling wood in Texas.
OAK	The second most popular wood, with a heavy smoke flavor, it's the official smoke of Texas brisket. Red oak, not yet available in pellets, is considered the best by many pit masters.	Good with red meat, pork, fish, and heavy game.
PECAN	Mild, nutty, similar to but milder than oak.	Good with any meats and known to add a more distinct smoke ring to beef.

THE FUTURE OF PELLETS

It's hard to predict what's next in pellet flavors. Special blends have become marketable for many pellet makers, but a lot of cooks like creating their own blends. Other than new blends (outlined in the chart here), the newest pellet "flavor" is charcoal. If you have a soft spot for traditional backyard grill flavor, this could be what you've been looking for. These black-colored pellets are best mixed with any regular wood pellet to enhance the smoke ring on your meat (charcoal's hotter combustion atmosphere aids in the creation of a more distinct smoke ring). Charcoal pellets also feature a hotter, cleaner burn than regular wood pellets.

🔥 Ring of Fire: The Coveted Smoke Ring

Smoke rings are thought of as one of the visual hallmarks of great barbecue. The reddish-pink color that develops close to the surface of the meat is a chemical reaction created by heat, smoke, and meat. Even at lower temperature settings, wood pellets release carbon dioxide and then, combined with the charred wood, create carbon monoxide and nitrogen dioxide. Those fumes result in a chemical reaction on the surface of the meat to slowly create that iconic reddish ring. Smoke rings don't affect flavor in the least, so don't obsess over them too much. Use pecan pellets or a nitrate-rich spice rub to enhance the ring.

FOOD-GRADE WOOD PELLET BLENDS

WOOD	BRAND(S)	FLAVOR	WHAT TO COOK WITH IT
APPLE MASH BLEND	CookinPellets	Lightly sweet blend of apple mash and hard maple	Great with light-flavor foods like chicken, pork, muffins, and cold-smoked dishes.
BBQ BLEND	Pit Boss	Sweet, savory, and tart blend of maple, hickory, and cherry	Good for all foods
BOURBON BROWN SUGAR	Cabela's	Seasoned oak blend of bourbon, smoke flavor, and sweetness	Good for beef, chicken, and pork
PELLET PRO EXCLUSIVE CHARCOAL BLEND	Smoke Daddy Inc.	Charcoal blended with red oak. Mix with any flavor of wood pellets and use to enhance smoke ring (see sidebar).	Good for all meats
COMPETITION BLEND	Pit Boss, Camp Chef, Lumber Jack, Cabela's, Louisiana Grills, Mojobricks, Q Pellets, Lowe's, Field & Stream, Dick's Sporting Goods, Walmart, Home Depot, HomComfort, Griller's Gold, Kingsford, and Traeger	Blend of sweet, savory, and tart (maple, hickory, and cherry)	Good for pork, chicken, and beef
PERFECT MIX BLEND	CookinPellets	Blend of hickory, cherry, hard maple, and apple	Great on short cooks; for any foods

WOOD	BRAND(S)	FLAVOR	WHAT TO COOK WITH IT
TEXAS BLEND	Green Mountain	Blend of oak, hickory, and mesquite	Good for all meats
REALTREE BIG GAME BLEND	Traeger	Blend of hickory, red and white oak, and rosemary	Great for venison, pheasant, and game meats
TURKEY PELLET BLEND WITH BRINE KIT	Traeger	Oak, hickory, maple, and rosemary	Turkey
TENNESSEE WHISKEY BARREL	Big Poppa Smokers, Louisiana Grills, Jack Daniels, Mr. Bar-B-Q	Aged oak from Jack Daniels Whiskey	Good for most meats

THE ART OF LOW-AND-SLOW SMOKING

Creating something as spectacular as smoked beef brisket is beautifully simple with a pellet smoker; however, it won't be quick. Here are the steps for a typical low-and-slow smoke:

1. Start cold—and clean. If your wood pellet grill smoker hasn't been used in a while, take a moment to remove the grate, drip pan, and heat deflector to clean out any residual ash (and extra pellets) from the cook chamber and fire pot with a shop vac.

2. Load your pellet hopper with your favorite hardwood pellet (oak is traditional for beef brisket). Replace the deflector, pans, and grate, and use your grill maker's preheating steps to ensure proper fuel flow.

3. Prep your beef. Wash your hands. When you are using smoke, great beef seasoning can be as simple as salt and pepper. It will take time for a large cut of meat like brisket to come to room temperature. Place the meat in the wood pellet grill smoker, and allow it to come fully off its chill and down to room temperature, and then up to cooking temperature (225°F in the cooking chamber). The cold meat may cause a temporary drop in your smoker temperature, but this is considered safer than leaving the meat out to come to room temperature
.

4. Place your temperature probe in the center of the thickest part of the meat.

5. Wash your hands again to allow for food-safe and clean operation of machinery. (This is something you'll repeat regularly!)

6. Adjust thermostat controls so your wood pellet grill maintains a cooking temperature of 225°F. Your brisket will need to cook at this low temperature for 1 hour and 30 minutes per pound of meat. Replenish the pellets in the hopper as needed, and allow your cook to go slowly if you want to achieve a distinct smoke ring.

7. Check and mop or spray the meat as desired. Mops and sprays are easy ways to add moisture to the surface of the meat. The liquid is typically a thinned-out version of your favorite sauce or fruit juice that is "mopped" on with a soft basting brush, or sprayed on from a reusable plastic kitchen spray bottle. Just don't open the door of the cooker more than absolutely necessary, especially during the first 1 hour and 30 minutes of cooking. Resist the urge to peek. Most wood pellet grills come with temperature probes that track the internal temperature of meat as it slowly cooks. This is a handy way to gauge progress without opening the grill.

8. When the meat reaches an internal temperature of 165°F, remind yourself that you are not done despite USDA recommendations! You may now opt to wrap, mop, or spritz hourly. Steady, low heat is the focus and smoke penetration is now secondary, as most of the flavor has been absorbed.

9 . Many pit masters swear by using pink butcher paper over aluminum foil to wrap brisket. The "Texas Crutch" is a somewhat derogatory term for wrapping the meat in aluminum foil during the rise from 165°F to 190°F. At times, the cooking can plateau and hit a point of resistance to an increase in internal temperature. That phenomenon is called "the stall" and varies from animal to animal. Wrapping in butcher paper or foil helps to break the stall, slowly braise the meat, and accelerates the fat and collagen breakdown that becomes pure succulence. That magic really kicks in once you hit 165°F and beyond.

10 . When the internal temperature hits 195°F, you can pull the roast from the wood pellet grill and allow the meat to rest for up to an hour before slicing. (Remember: The meat will continue to cook for a few minutes after being removed.) The rest period allows juices to soak into the meat rather than drain quickly due to a premature carving.

11 . During the rest, take time to make sure you are properly running the pellet cooker through its important shutdown cycle so you know your smoker will be primed and ready for the next cook.

UP IN SMOKE

Smoking isn't just for preserving any more. These days, it's common to see smoked turkey and cheeses in supermarkets because people love the flavor. And, though brisket, ribs, and chicken are popular favorites, the good taste isn't limited to meats. Smoked vegetables, nuts, and even fruit are becoming mainstream delicacies.

CUTS OF BEEF AND PORK

BEEF

1. Neck
2. Chuck
3. Rib
4. Short Loin
5. Sirloin
6. Tenderloin
7. Top Sirloin
8. Rump Cap
9. Round
10. Brisket
11. Shoulder C
12. Short Plate
13. Flank

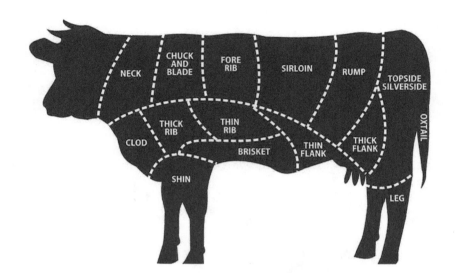

PORK

1. Head
2. Clear Plate
3. Back Fat
4. Boston Butt/Shoulde
5. Loin
6. Ham
7. Cheek
8. Picnic Shoulder
9. Ribs
10. Bacon
11. Hock

FAVORITE FOODS TO SMOKE ON A WOOD PELLET GRILL

ITEM TO SMOKE	SMOKING TEMP.	SMOKING TIME	INTERNAL TEMP.	TYPE OF WOOD CHIPS
CHICKEN				
CHICKEN (BONELESS, SKINLESS)	350°F	25 TO 30 MINUTES	170°F	ALDER, PECAN
CHICKEN CUT UP (LEGS/ THIGHS/ BREASTS)	250°F	1 HOUR 30 MINUTES TO 2 HOURS	165°F	CHERRY, PECAN, OAK, APPLE, MAPLE
CHICKEN OR TURKEY (GROUND)	275°F	1 HOUR TO 1 HOUR 30 MINUTES	160°F	APPLE
CHICKEN WINGS	350°F	50 TO 60 MINUTES	165°F	HICKORY, OAK
CH1CKEN, \VHOLE(3TO 4 POUNDS)	250°F	45 minutes per pound	165°F	CHERRY, PECAN, OAK, APPLE
CHICKEN HALVES	250°F	3 HOURS	165°F	CHERRY
JERK CHICKEN LEG QUARTERS	275°F	1 HOUR 30 MINUTES	165°F	MESQUITE AND A FEW WHOLE PIMENTO (ALL-SPICE) BERRIES
TURKEY				
TURKEY (WHOLE)	250°F	30 MINUTES PER POUND	165°F	APPLE
TURKEY LEGS	225°F	4 TO 5 HOURS	165°F	APPLE
PORK				
BABY BACK RIBS	225°F	5 HOURS 30 MINUTES TO 6 HOURS	190°F	HICKORY
BRATS	22S°F	1 HOUR 30 MINUTES TO 2 HOURS	160°F	OAK, PECAN, HICKORY
PORK SHOULDER BOSTON BUTI (PULLED)	22S°F	8 TO 9 HOURS	205°F	HICKORY
PORK SAUSAGE (GROUND)	225°F	2 HOURS	165°F	APPLE
PORK CHOPS	325°F	45 TO 50 MINUTES	160°F	OAK, HICKORY,APPLE
PORK LOIN ROAST	250°F	3 HOURS	160°F	APPLE, HICKORY
PORK SPARE RIBS	250°F	6 HOURS	190°F	MESQUITE, CHER-RY
PORK TENDERLOIN	225°F	2 HOURS TO 2 HOURS 30 MINUTES	160°F	HICKORY, APPLE

ITEM TO SMOKE	SMOKING TEMP.	SMOKING TIME	INTERNAL TEMP.	TYPE OF WOOD CHIPS
BEEF				
BRISKET	225°F	1 HOUR TO 1 HOUR 30 MINUTES	195°F TO 205°F	OAK
CHUCK ROAST	225°F	1 HOUR PER POUND	L 20°F TO L55°F	OAK, MESQUITE
HAMBURGERS	425°F	20 TO 25 MINUTES	160°F	OAK
FILET MIGNON	450°F	12 TO 14 MINUTES	"120°F RARE 135°F MEDIUM I55°F WELL DONE"	OAK, PECAN
FLANK STEAK	450°F	8 to 20 minutes	"120°F RARE 135°F MEDIUM I55°F WELL DONE"	ANY
FLAT IRON STEAK	450°F	8 TO 20 MINUTES	"120°F RARE 135°F MEDIUM I55°F WELL DONE"	ANY
LONDON BROIL(TOP ROUND)	350°F	12 TO 16 MINUTES	"120°F RARE 135°F MEDIUM I55°F WELL DONE"	ANY
PRIME RIB	450°F TO SEAR, 300°F TO SMOKE	20 MINUTES PER POUND	"120°F RARE 135°F MEDIUM I55°F WELL DONE"	OAK, PECAN
RIBEYE	450°F	8 TO 20 MINUTES	"120°F RARE 135°F MEDIUM I55°F WELL DONE"	HICKORY,OAK, MESQUITE
RUMP ROAST	225°F	1 HOUR PER POUND	"120°F RARE 135°F MEDIUM I55°F WELL DONE"	OAK, MESQUITE
SHORT RIBS (BEEF)	225°F	3 TO 4 HOUR	"120°F RARE 135°F MEDIUM I55°F WELL DONE"	OAK, MESQUITE
SIRLOIN TIP ROAST	225°F	1 HOUR PER POUND	"120°F RARE 135°F MEDIUM I55°F WELL DONE"	OAK, MESQUITE
T-BONE AND PORTERHOUSE STEAKS	165°F, 450°F	45 TO 50 MINUTES	"120°F RARE 135°F MEDIUM I55°F WELL DONE"	HICKORY
TENDERLOIN (BEEF)	400°F	25 TO 30 MINUTES	"120°F RARE 135°F MEDIUM I55°F WELL DONE"	OAK, HICKORY, PECAN
TEXAS SHOULDER	250°F	12 TO 16 HOURS	195°F	OAK CLOD
TRI-TIP	420°F	45 MINUTES TO 1 HOUR	"120°F RARE 135°F MEDIUM I55°F WELL DONE"	OAK HOUR

ITEM TO SMOKE	SMOKING TEMP.	SMOKING TIME	INTERNAL TEMP.	TYPE OF WOOD CHIPS
FISH AND SEAFOOD				
FISH (HALIBUT,SEABASS, WORDFISH,TROUT, AND COD)	200°F TO 225°F	1 HOUR 30 MINUTES TO 2 HOURS	140°F	ALDER,APPLE,CHERRY,OAKALDER,APPLE,CHERRY,OAK
OYSTERS	225°F	15 TO 20 MINUTES	TO TASTE	APPLE,CHERRY, OAK
SALMON	250°F	1 TO 2 HOURS	145°F	ALDER
TUNA STEAKS	250°F	1 HOUR 30 MINUTES TO 2 HOURS	125°F	APPLE,CHERRY, ,OAK
FRUIT AND VEGETABLES				
BELL PEPPERS	225°F	1 HOUR 30 MINUTES	UNTIL TENDER	MAPLE
CAULIFLOWER	200°F TO 250°F	45 MINUTES TO 1 HOUR 30 MINUTES	UNTIL TENDER	MAPLE
CORN ON THECOB	450°F	12 TO 14 MINUTES	UNTILTENDER	HICKORY,OAK, PECAN, MESQUITE
JALAPENO PEPPERS	250°F	1 HOUR TO 1 HOUR 30 MINUTES	UNTIL TENDER	MAPLE
ONIONS	250°F	2 HOURS	UNTIL TENDER	MAPLE, MES-QUITE
PEACHES	225°F	35 TO 45 MINUTES	TO TASTE	MAPLE
PINEAPPLE	250°F	1 HOUR TO 1 HOUR 30 MINUTES	TO TASTE	MAPLE
POTATOES	400°F	L HOUR 15 MINUTES	UNTIL TENDER	MAPLE,PECAN
SWEET POTATOES, WHOLE	375°F	1 HOUR TO 1 HOUR 30 MINUTES	UNTIL TENDER	MAPLE
SQUASH AND ZUCCHINI	225°F	1 HOUR	UNTIL TENDER	MAPLE

UNUSUAL FOODS TO SMOKE ON A WOOD PELLET GRILL

ITEM TO SMOKE	SMOKING TEMP.	SMOKING TIME	INTERNAL TEMP.	TYPE OF WOOD PELLETS
ALLIGATOR	225°F	2 HOURS	165°F	MESQUITE
ARTICHOKES	225°F	2 HOURS	TO TASTE	MAPLE
ASPARAGUS	240°F	1 HOUR	TO TASTE	MAPLE
BACON OR CANDIED BACON	225°F	30 TO 45 MINUTES	140°F	HICKORY, MAPLE
BAKED BEANS	300°F	2 hours 30 minutes to 3 hours	UNTIL BUBBLY	HICKORY, OAK, MESQUITE
BEEF JERKY (THIN SLICED BEEF BOTTOM ROUND)	180°F	4 TO 5 HOURS	TO TASTE	HICKORY
BISON BURGERS	425°F	17 TO 19 MINUTES	140°F TO 160°F	MESQUITE, BBQ BLEND
BOLOGNA	250°F	1 HOUR	TO TASTE	HICKORY
BROWNIES	350°F	23 TO 28 MINUTES	UNTIL A TOOTH-PICK INSERTED COMES OUT CLEAN	APPLE, CHERRY
CABBAGE	240°F	2 HOURS	TO TASTE	OAK, MAPLE, APPLE
CAKE	350°F	1 HOUR	UNTIL A TOOTH-PICK INSERTED COMES OUT CLEAN	APPLE, CHERRY
CHEESES	UNDER 90°F	30 TO 45 MINUTES	TO TASTE	APPLE, HICKO-RY, MESQUITE
COBBLER	375°F	20 TO 25 MINUTES	UNTIL BROWN AND BUBBLY	APPLE, CHERRY
COOKIES	375°F	10 TO 12 MINUTES	UNTIL LIGHTLY BROWNED	ALDER, PECAN
CORNBREAD	375°F	25 TO 35 MINUTES	UNTIL A TOOTH-PICK INSERTED COMES OUT CLEAN	OAK, APPLE, PECAN

ITEM TO SMOKE	SMOKING TEMP.	SMOKING TIME	INTERNAL TEMP.	TYPE OF WOOD PELLETS
CORNED BEEF/PASTRAMI	275°F	4 TO 5 HOURS	185°F	OAK, HICKORY
CORNISH GAME HENS (APPROXIMATELY 2½ POUNDS EACH)	275°F	2 TO 3 HOURS OR 45 MINUTES PER POUND	170°F	APPLE
CRAB	200°F	15 MINUTES PER POUND	TO TASTE	OAK
DUCK, WHOLE (5 POUNDS)	250°F	4 HOURS	165°F	CHERRY, PECAN
EGGPLANT	200°F	1 hour to 1 hour 30 minutes	TO TASTE	MAPLE
GARLIC	225°F	2 HOURS	TO TASTE	OAK
GOOSE BACON	165°F FIRST COOK, 250°F SECOND COOK	4 HOURS 15 MINUTES	TO TASTE	CHERRY
HAM, PRE-COOKED (5 TO 7 POUNDS)	275°F	5 HOURS	160°F	CHERRY
HARD-BOILED EGGS (FOR DEVILED EGGS)	200°F	20 TO 30 MINUTES	TO TASTE	HICKORY
ICE CREAM BREAD	350°F	50 TO 60 MINUTES	UNTIL A TOOTH-PICK INSERTED COMES OUT CLEAN	APPLE, CHERRY
KIELBASA SAUSAGE	225°F	1 HOUR 30 MINUTES TO 2 HOURS	160°F	OAK, PECAN, HICKORY
LAMB CHOPS	165°F TO SMOKE, 450°F TO SEAR	10 TO 20 MINUTES	145°F	CHERRY
LAMB RACK, 7 OR 8 (4-OUNCE) CHOPS	275°F	1 HOUR 30 MINUTES TO 2 HOURS	145°F	APPLE, CHERRY, OAK
CROWN (2 RACKS UPRIGHT AND TIED TOGETHER TO FORM A CROWN)				
LEG OF LAMB	325°F	20 TO 25 MINUTES PER POUND	145°F	APPLE, OAK
LOBSTER TAIL	225°F	45 MINUTES TO 1 HOUR	130° TO 140°F	ALDER, OAK
LOX	80°F	6 HOURS	TO TASTE	ALDER
MAC AND CHEESE	225°F	1 HOUR	UNTIL BUBBLY	HICKORY, MESQUITE
MEATLOAF	225°F	2 HOURS	165°F	HICKORY, MESQUITE, OAK

ITEM TO SMOKE	SMOKING TEMPERAT	SMOKING TIME	INTERNAL TEMPERATURE	TYPE OF WOOD PELLETS
MUFFINS	375°F	25 TO 30 MINUTES	UNTIL A TOOTH-PICK INSERTED COMES OUT CLEAN	APPLE, CHERRY
MUSHROOMS	225°F	1 HOUR 30 MINUTES	TO TASTE	OAK
MUSSELS	150°F TO 180°F	1 HOUR 30 MINUTES	TO TASTE	ALDER, CHERRY
NUTS	225°F	1 HOUR	TO TASTE	HICKORY, MES-QUITE
PHEASANT	250°F	3 TO 4 HOURS	160°F	APPLE, CHERRY, HICKORY
QUAIL	225°F	1 HOUR	145°F	HICKORY
SCALLOPS	225°F	25 MINUTES	UNTIL OPAQUE/ FIRM	CHERRY, OAK
SHRIMP (RAW)	450°F	4 TO 6 MINUTES	UNTIL PINK	MESQUITE, HICK-ORY, PECAN
SNACK MIX	225°F	2 HOURS TO 2 HOURS 30 MINUTES	UNTIL DRY	HICKORY, MES-QUITE
TOMATOES	200°F	45 MINUTES	TO TASTE	OAK
TURDUCKEN	275°F	2 HOURS	165°F	OAK, CHERRY
VENISON	225°F	1 HOUR 20 MINUTES	130° TO 140°F	HICKORY

Wood Pellet Tips

Before getting started with your Wood Pellet for the first time, here are some of the most important things you need to know about Wood Pellets.

Wood pellets are a form of compressed wood and sawdust created through the process of exposing specific agents to a certain degree of heat. And one of the most well-known uses of wood pellets is to use it to fuel certain cooking smokers and grills.

Wood Pellet Smokers and Grills are known for bringing an exceptional smoked flavor of wood to the food ingredients you smoke or any type of meat. And the smoking taste that you can get from wood pellet smokers is unique that you can never forget the taste of food once you try it.

They are mainly characterized by being eco-friendly because most of the Wood Pellets are made of renewable elements and materials. The production of Wood Pellets encourages the process of repurposing the materials that can be thrown away by people. They are usually available in various forms and types, each of which can offer a different flavor.

Wood pellets are known for being a lot more efficient than other types of gas and fossil because wood pellets are mainly able to use about 90% of the contained energy. And then the wood pellets can turn the energy into heat.

Wood pellets can help you cook some very delicious dishes with the smoky flavor it can offer you. Thanks to the Wood Pellet Smoking method, you will be able to enjoy tastes like those obtained when using charcoal.

They can help you produce a very nice flavor, and you will be able to easily clean you Wood Pellet Smoker or Grill because there won't be so much ash.

Whenever you want to use your wood pellet smoker grill, switch on the charcoal grill by adding up a charcoal quantity. Then wait for the charcoal to heat up before sprinkling several wood pellets under the rock grate.

Within a short period, your wood pellets will start igniting. And once you see the pellets sparkle, it is a signal that you should start cooking, and you will see the nice wood smoke. To keep the smoke, close the lid of your wood pellet smoker.

A pellet tube smoker is also used to keep wood pellets as you combine it with the charcoal. And this can help increase the smokiness of the flavor.

Selecting a Smoker

You need to invest in a good smoker if you are going to smoke meat regularly. Consider these options when buying a smoker. Here are two natural fire option for you:

Charcoal smokers

It is fueled by a combination of charcoal and wood. Charcoal burns quickly, and the temperature remains steady so that you won't have any problem with a charcoal smoker. The wood gives a great flavor to the meat, and you will enjoy smoking meats.

Wood smokers

The wood smoker will give your brisket and ribs the best smoky flavor and taste, but it is a bit harder to cook with wood. Both hardwood blocks and chips are used as fuel.

Choose Your Wood

Choose your wood carefully because the type of wood you will use affects the flavor and taste of the meat significantly. Here are a few options for you:

·   Maple: Maple has a smoky and sweet taste and goes well with pork or poultry

·   Alder: Alder is sweet and light. Perfect for poultry and fish.

·   Apple: Apple has a mild and sweet flavor. That goes well with pork, fish, and poultry.

·   Oak: Oak is excellent for slow cooking. Ideal for game, pork, beef, and lamb.

·   Mesquite: It is a smoky flavor and strong that goes well with pork or beef.

·   Hickory: Has a smoky and strong flavor. It goes well with beef and lamb.

·   Cherry: It has a mild and sweet flavor. Great for pork, beef, and turkey

Chart to Support You with Selecting the Best Wood Chips

Wood Type	Fish	Chicken	Beef	Pork
Annie	Yes	Yes	No	No
Alder	Yes	Yes	No	Yes
Cherry	Yes	Yes	Yes	Yes
Hickory	No	No	Yes	Yes
Maple	No	Yes	No	No
Mulberry	Yes	Yes	No	Yes
Mesauite	No	No	Yes	Yes
Oak	Yes	Yes	Yes	Yes
Pecan	No	Yes	Yes	Yes
Pear	No	Yes	No	Yes
Peach	No	Yes	No	Yes
Walnut	No	No	Yes	Yes

Remember, *black smoke is harmful, and white smoke is good. Ensure proper ventilation for great tasting smoked meat.*

Find the Right Temperature Chips

- *Start at 250°F (120°C): Start your smoker a bit hot.*
- *Once you add the meat to the smoker, it will drop, which is fine.*
- *Maintain the temperature. Monitor and maintain temperature. Keep the temperature steady during the smoking process.*

Avoid peeking now and then. Smoke and heat two most crucial element make your meat taste great. If you open the cover now and then lose both, your meat loses flavor. Only the lid only when you genuinely need it. Smoking is a very indirect method of cooking that relies on some different factors to give you the most perfectly cooked meal that you are looking for. Each of the components is very important to the whole process as they all work together to create the meal of your dreams.

Time

Unlike grilling or even Barbequing, smoking takes a long time and requires a lot of patience. It takes time for the smoky flavor to get infused into the meats slowly. It takes about 8 minutes to thoroughly cook a steak through direct heating, while smoking (indirect heat) will take around 35-40 minutes.

Temperature

When it comes to smoking, the temperature is affected by many different factors that are not only limited to the wind, cold air temperatures, but also the cooking wood's dryness. Some smokers work best with large fires controlled by the draw of a chimney and restricted airflow through the various vents of the cooking chamber and firebox.

Most smokers are designed to work at temperatures as low as 180°F to as high as 300°F. But the recommend temperature usually falls between 250°F and 275°F.

Airflow

The air level to which the fire is exposed greatly determines how your fire will burn and how quickly it will burn the fuel. For instance, if you restrict airflow into the firebox by closing the available vents, the fire will burn at a low temperature and vice versa.

Typically, in smokers, after lighting up the fire, the vents are opened to allow for maximum airflow. They are then adjusted throughout the cooking process to make sure that optimum flame is achieved.

Insulation

Insulation is also essential when it comes to smokers as it helps to easily manage the cooking process throughout the whole cooking session. Good insulation allows smokers to efficiently reach the desired temperature instead of waiting for hours upon hours.

CHAPTER 3

Appetizers and Sides Recipes

Smashed Potato Casserole

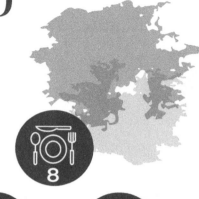

NUTRITION

Calories: 232 Fat: 2g
Carbs: 48g Protein: 9g

8

45 - 60 MINUTES

30 MINUTES

INTOLERANCES:

Gluten-Free
Egg-Free

SHOPPING LIST

- 1 small red onion, thinly sliced
- 1 small green bell pepper, thinly sliced
- 1 small red bell pepper, thinly sliced
- ¾ cup sour cream

- 1 small yellow bell pepper, thinly sliced
- 3 cups mashed potatoes
- 8 - 10 bacon
- ¼ cup bacon grease or salted butter (½ stick)

- 1 ½ teaspoons barbecue rub
- 3 cups shredded sharp cheddar cheese (divided)
- 4 cups hash brown potatoes (frozen)

DIRECTIONS

1. Get that bacon cooking over medium heat in a large skillet. Cook till nice and crisp. Aim for 5 minutes on both sides. Then set aside your bacon. Pour the bacon grease into a glass container and set aside.
2. Using the same skillet, warm up the butter or bacon grease over medium heat. When warm enough, sauté bell peppers and red onions. You're aiming for al dente. When done, set it all aside.
3. Grab a casserole dish, preferably one that is 9 by 11 inches. Spray with some nonstick cooking spray, then spread the mashed potatoes out, covering the entire bottom of the dish.
4. Add the sour cream to the next layer over the potatoes. When you're done, season it with some of the barbecue rub.
5. Create a new layer with the sautéed veggies over the potatoes.
6. Sprinkle your sharp cheddar cheese—just 1½ of the cups.

Then add the frozen hash brown potatoes.
7. Scoop out the rest of the bacon grease or butter from the sautéed veggies, all over the hash browns, and then top it all off with some delicious crumbled bacon bits. Set up your wood pellet smoker grill for indirect cooking. Preheat to 350°F. Use whatever pellets you like.
8. Add the rest of the sharp cheddar cheese (1½ cups) over the whole thing, and then use some aluminum foil to cover the casserole dish.
9. Set up your wood pellet smoker grill for indirect cooking. Preheat to 350°F. Use whatever pellets you like.
10. Let the whole thing bake for 45 - 60 minutes. Ideally, you want the cheese to bubble.
11. Take it out and let it sit for about 10 minutes.
12. Serve!

Buffalo Mini Sausages

 **NUTRITION**

Calories: 198, Fat: 17g
Cholesterol: 48mg, Carbs: 3g,
Protein: 8g

 INTOLERANCES:

Egg-Free

10

1hr - 30
MINUTES

30
MINUTES

 SHOPPING LIST

- 8 ounces regular cream cheese (room temp)
- ¾ cup cheddar cheese blend and shredded Monterey Jack (not necessary)
- 1 teaspoon smoked paprika
- 1 teaspoon garlic powder
- ½ teaspoon red pepper flakes (not necessary)
- ¾ cup sour cream
- Little Smokies sausages (20)
- 10 bacon strips, thinly sliced and halved
- 10 jalapeno peppers (medium)

 DIRECTIONS

1. Wash the jalapenos, then slice them up along the length. Get a spoon, or a paring knife if you prefer, and use that to take out the seeds and the veins.
2. Place the scooped-out jalapenos on a veggie grilling tray and put it all aside.
3. Get a small bowl and mix the shredded cheese, cream cheese, paprika, cayenne pepper, garlic powder, and red pepper flakes. Mix them thoroughly.
4. Get your jalapenos which you've hollowed out, and then stuff them with the cream cheese mix.
5. Get your little Smokies sausage, and then put it right onto each of the cheese stuffed jalapenos.
6. Grab some of the thinly sliced and halved bacon strips and wrap them around each of the stuffed jalapenos and their sausage.
7. Grab some toothpicks. Use them to keep the bacon nicely secured to the sausage.
8. Set up your wood pellet smoker grill so it's ready for indirect cooking. Get it preheated to 250°F. Use hickory or blends for your wooden pellets.
9. Put your jalapeno peppers in and smoke them at 250°F for anywhere from 90 minutes to 120 minutes. You want to keep it going until the bacon is nice and crispy.
10. Take out the atomic buffalo turds, and then let them rest for about 5 minutes.
11. Serve!

Brisket Baked Beans

 NUTRITION

Calories: 200, Fat: 2g, Cholesterol: 10mg, Carbs: 35g, Protein: 9g

 INTOLERANCES:

Gluten-Free, Egg-Free, Lactose-Free

20 MINUTES

1hr - 20 MINUTES

10

 SHOPPING LIST

- 1 green bell pepper (medium, diced)
- 1 red bell pepper (medium, diced)
- 1 yellow onion (large, diced)
- 2 - 6 jalapeno peppers (diced)
- 1 can baked

- 2 tablespoons olive oil (extra-virgin)
- 3 cups brisket flat (chopped) beans (28 ounces)
- 1 can red kidney beans (1 4ounces, rinsed, drained)
- 1 cup barbecue sauce

- ½ cup brown sugar (packed)
- 2 teaspoons mustard (ground)
- 3 cloves of garlic (chopped)
- 1 ½ teaspoon black pepper
- 1 ½ teaspoon kosher salt

DIRECTIONS

1. Put a skillet on the fire, on medium heat. Warm up your olive oil. Toss in the diced jalapenos, peppers, and onions. Stir every now and then for 8 minutes.
2. Grab a 4-quart casserole dish. Now, in your dish, mix in the pork and beans, kidney beans, baked beans, chopped brisket, cooked peppers and onions, brown sugar, barbecue sauce, garlic, mustard, salt, and black pepper.
3. Set up your wood pellet smoker grill so it's ready for indirect cooking.

4. Preheat your grill to 325°F, using whatever pellets you want.
5. Cook your brisket beans on the grill, for 90 minutes to 120 minutes. Keep it uncovered as you cook. When it's ready, you'll know, because the beans will get thicker and will have bubbles as well.
6. Rest the food for 15 minutes, before you finally move on to step number 5.
7. Serve!

Twice-Baked Spaghetti Squash

NUTRITION

Calories: 214, Fat: 3g,
Cholesterol: 17mg, Carbs: 27g
Protein: 16g

INTOLERANCES:

Egg-Free

15 MINUTES

1 hr

2

SHOPPING LIST

- 1 spaghetti squash (medium)
- 1 tablespoon olive oil (extra virgin)
- 1 teaspoon salt
- ½ teaspoon pepper
- ½ cup Parmesan cheese (grated, divided)
- divided)
- ½ cup mozzarella cheese (shredded, divided)

DIRECTIONS

1. Cut the squash along the length in half. Make sure you're using a knife that's large enough, and sharp enough. Once you're done, take out the pulp and the seeds from each half with a spoon.
2. Rub the insides of each half of the squash with some olive oil. When you're done with that, sprinkle the salt and pepper.
3. Set up your wood pellet smoker grill for indirect cooking.
4. Preheat your grill to 375°F with your preferred wood pellets.
5. Put each half of the squash on the grill. Make sure they're both facing upwards on the grill grates, which

should be nice and hot.
6. Bake for 45 minutes, keeping it on the grill until the internal temperature of the squash hits 170°F. You'll know you're done when you find it easy to pierce the squash with a fork.
7. Move the squash to your cutting board. Let it sit there for 10 minutes, so it can cool a bit.
8. Turn up the temp on your wood pellet smoker grill to 425°F.
9. Use a fork to remove the flesh from the squash in strands by raking it back and forth. Do be careful, because you want the shells to remain intact. The strands you rake

off should look like spaghetti, if you're doing it right.

10. Put the spaghetti squash strands in a large bowl, and then add in half of your mozzarella and half of your Parmesan cheeses. Combine them by stirring.

11. Take the mix, and stuff it into the squash shells. When you're done, sprinkle them with the rest of the Parmesan and mozzarella cheeses.

12. Optional: You can top these with some bacon bits, if you like.

13. Allow the stuffed spaghetti squash shells you've now stuffed to bake at 435°F for 15 minutes, or however long it takes the cheese to go brown.

14. Serve and enjoy.

Bacon-Wrapped Asparagus

NUTRITION

Calories: 71, Fat: 3g,
Carbs: 1g, Protein: 6g

INTOLERANCES:

Gluten-Free, Egg-Free,
Lactose-Free

15 MINUTES

25-30 MINUTES

6

SHOPPING LIST

- 15 - 20 spears of fresh asparagus (1 pound)
- Olive oil (extra virgin)
- 5 slices bacon (thinly sliced)
- 1 teaspoon salt and pepper (or your preferred rub)

DIRECTIONS

1. Break off the ends of the asparagus, then trim it all so they're down to the same length.
2. Separate the asparagus into bundles—3 spears per bundle. Then spritz them with some olive oil.
3. Use a piece of bacon to wrap up each bundle. When you're done, lightly dust the wrapped bundle with some salt and pepper to taste, or your preferred rub.
4. Set up your wood pellet smoker grill so that it's ready for indirect cooking.
5. Put some fiberglass mats on your grates. Make sure they're the fiberglass kind. This will keep your asparagus from getting stuck on your grill gates.
6. Preheat your grill to 400°F, with whatever pellets you prefer. You can do this as you prep your asparagus.
7. Grill the wraps for 25 minutes to 30 minutes, tops. The goal is to get your asparagus looking nice and tender, and the bacon deliciously crispy.

Garlic Parmesan Wedges

 NUTRITION

Calories: 194, Fat: 5g
Cholesterol: 5mg, Carbs: 32g
Protein: 5g

INTOLERANCES:

Gluten-Free, Egg-Free

SHOPPING LIST

- 3 russet potatoes (large)
- 2 teaspoons of garlic powder
- ¾ teaspoon black pepper
- 1 ½ teaspoons of salt
- ¾ cup Parmesan cheese (grated)
- 3 tablespoons fresh cilantro (chopped, optional. You can replace this with flat-leaf parsley)
- ½ cup blue cheese (per serving, as optional dip. Can be replaced with ranch dressing)

DIRECTIONS

1. Use some cold water to scrub your potatoes as gently as you can with a veggie brush. When done, let them dry.
2. Slice your potatoes along the length in half. Cut each half into a third.
3. Get all the extra moisture off your potato by wiping it all away with a paper towel. If you don't do this, then you're not going to have crispy wedges!
4. In a large bowl, throw in your potato wedges, some olive oil, garlic powder, salt, garlic, and pepper, and then toss them with your hands, lightly. You want to make sure the spices and oil get on every wedge.
5. Place your wedges on a nonstick grilling tray, or pan, or basked. The single layer kind. Make sure it's at least 15 x 12 inches.
6. Set up your wood pellet smoker grill so it's ready for indirect cooking.
7. Preheat your grill to 425°F, with whatever wood pellets you like.
8. Set the grilling tray upon your preheated grill. Roast the wedges for 15 minutes before you flip them. Once you turn them, roast them for another 15 minutes, or 20 tops. The outside should

be a nice, crispy, golden brown.

9. Sprinkle your wedges generously with the Parmesan cheese. When you're done, garnish it with some parsley, or cilantro, if you like. Serve these bad boys up with some ranch dressing, or some blue cheese, or just eat them that way!

 15 MINUTES 35 MINUTES 3

Grilled Chili Lime Chicken

 NUTRITION

Calories: 194, Fat: 5g
Cholesterol: 5mg, Carbs: 32g
Protein: 5g

INTOLERANCES:

Gluten-Free, Egg-Free

SHOPPING LIST

- ¼ cup fresh lime juice
- One lime, zested
- One teaspoon red pepper flakes
- Half teaspoon ground cumin
- One teaspoon salt
- One teaspoon brown sugar
- Four medium skinless, boneless chicken breast halves
- Two tablespoons chopped fresh cilantro
- Two tablespoons olive oil
- Two cloves garlic, minced

10 MINUTES   10 MINUTES   4

 DIRECTIONS

1. First, take a little bowl and whisk lime juice, lime zest, cumin, olive oil, brown sugar, garlic, salt, and red pepper flakes. Add chicken in the bowl or big plastic bag and then add the lime marinade. Seal the bag and wrap the bowl and keep in the freezer to preserve for a half-hour to one day.

2. Now, preheat grill middle to high heat and lightly oil the grate.

3. Add chicken breasts on the preheated grill and fry until it gets white in the middle and the skin gets golden and lightly charred. Cook approx five minutes per side.

4. Move chicken breast to the plate and allow stand for five minutes and cut and decorate with cilantro.

Hickory Smoked Moink Ball Skewers

SHOPPING LIST

- ½ pound pork sausage (ground)
- •½ pound ground beef (80% lean)
- 1 egg (large)
- ½ cup red onions (minced)
- ½ cup Parmesan cheese (grated)
- ½ cup Italian breadcrumbs
- ¼ cup parsley (finely chopped)
- ¼ cup milk (whole)
- 2 garlic cloves (minced) or 1 teaspoon garlic (crushed)
- 1 teaspoon oregano
- ½ teaspoon kosher salt
- ½ teaspoon black pepper
- ¼ cup barbecue sauce
- ½ pound bacon slices (thinly sliced, halved)

DIRECTIONS

1. Mix up the ground pork sausage, ground beef, breadcrumbs, onion, egg, parsley, Parmesan cheese, garlic, milk, oregano, salt, and pepper in a large bowl. Whatever you do, don't overwork your meat.
2. Make meatballs of 1½ ounces each. They should be about 1½ in width. Put them on your Teflon-coated fiberglass mat.
3. Wrap up each meatball in half a slice of your thinly sliced bacon.
4. Spear your moink balls, three to a skewer.
5. Set up your wood pellet smoker grill so that it's nice and ready for indirect cooking.
6. Preheat your grill to 225°F, with your hickory wood pellets.
7. Smoke the skewered moink balls for

half an hour.

8. Turn up the temperature to 350°F, and keep it that way until the internal temperature of your skewered moink balls hits 175°F, which should take about 40 to 45 minutes, max.

9. When the bacon gets nice and crispy, brush your moink balls with whatever barbecue sauce you like. Ideally, you should do this in the last five minutes of your cook time.

10. Serve the moink ball skewers while they're hot.

Bacon Cheddar Slider

SHOPPING LIST

- 1 pound ground beef (80% lean)
- 1/2 teaspoon of garlic salt
- 1/2 teaspoon salt
- 1/2 teaspoon of garlic
- 1/2 teaspoon onion
- 1/2 teaspoon black
- pepper
- 6 bacon slices, cut in half
- 1/2 Cup mayonnaise
- 2 teaspoons of creamy wasabi (optional)
- 6 (1 oz) sliced sharp cheddar cheese, cut in
- half (optional)
- Sliced red onion
- 1/2 Cup sliced kosher dill pickles
- 12 mini breads sliced horizontally
- Ketchup

DIRECTIONS

1. Place ground beef, garlic salt, seasoned salt, garlic powder, onion powder and black hupe pepper in a medium bowl.
2. Divide the meat mixture into 12 equal parts, shape into small thin round patties (about 2 ounces each) and save.
3. Cook the bacon on medium heat over medium heat for 5-8 minutes until crunchy. Set aside.
4. To make the sauce, mix the mayonnaise and horseradish in a small bowl, if used.
5. Preheat wood pellet smoker grill to 350°F using selected pellets. Griddle surface should be approximately 400°F.
6. Spray a cooking spray on the griddle cooking surface for best non-stick results.
7. Grill the putty for 3-4 minutes each until the internal temperature reaches 160°F.
8. If necessary, place a sharp cheddar cheese slice on each patty while the patty is on the griddle or after the patty is removed from the griddle.
9. Place a small amount of mayonnaise mixture, a slice of red onion, and a hamburger pate in the lower half of each roll. Pickled slices, bacon and ketchup.

'Shrooms and Crab

📖 NUTRITION

Calories: 60, Fat: 4g, Cholesterol: 20mg, Carbs: 2g,Protein: 2g

📖 INTOLERANCES:

Egg-Free

🧺 SHOPPING LIST

- 6 medium-sized portobello mushrooms
- Extra virgin olive oil
- 1/3 Grated parmesan cheese cup
- Club Beat Staffing:
- 8 oz fresh crab meat or canned or imitation crab meat
- 2 tablespoons extra virgin
- olive oil
- 1/3 Chopped celery
- Chopped red peppers
- 1/2 cup chopped green onion
- 1/2 cup Italian breadcrumbs
- 1/2 Cup mayonnaise
- 8 oz cream cheese at room temperature
- 1/2 teaspoon of garlic
- 1 tablespoon dried parsley
- Grated parmesan cheese cup
- 1 1 teaspoon of Old Bay seasoning
- 1/4 teaspoon of kosher salt
- 1/4 teaspoon black pepper

🛍 DIRECTIONS

1. Clean the mushroom cap with a damp paper towel. Cut off the stem and save it.
2. Remove the brown gills from the bottom of the mushroom cap with a spoon and discard.
3. Prepare crab meat stuffing. If you are using canned crab meat, drain, rinse, and remove shellfish.
4. Heat the olive oil in a frying pan over medium high heat. Add celery, peppers and green onions and fry for 5 minutes. Set aside for cooling.
5. Gently pour the chilled sautéed vegetables and the remaining ingredients into a large bowl.
6. Cover and refrigerate crab meat stuffing until ready to use.
7. Put the crab mixture in each mushroom cap and make a mound in the center.
8. Sprinkle extra virgin olive oil and sprinkle parmesan cheese on each stuffed mushroom cap. Put the mushrooms in a 10 x 15-inch baking dish.

9. Use the pellets to set the wood pellet smoker grill to indirect heating and preheat to 375°F.
10. Bake for 30-45 minutes until the filling becomes hot (165°F as measured by an instant-read digital thermometer) and the mushrooms begin to release juice.

Parmesan Tomatoes

 NUTRITION

Calories: 130,   Carbs: 9g,

Fat: 8g   Protein: 6g

 INTOLERANCES:

Gluten-Free, Egg-Free

 10 MINUTES
 10 MINUTES
 6

SHOPPING LIST

- 9 halved Tomatoes
- 1 cup grated Parmesan cheese
- 1/2 tsp. Ground black pepper
- 1/4 tsp. Onion powder
- 1 tbsp. Dried rosemary
- 2 tbsps. Olive oil
- 5 minced Garlic cloves
- 1 tsp. Kosher salt

DIRECTIONS

1. Heat a grill to medium-low heat and oil grates.
2. Place tomatoes halves cut side down, onto the grill and cook for 5-7 minutes.
3. Heat olive oil in a pan over a medium heat. Add garlic, rosemary, black pepper, onion powder, and salt and cook for 3-5 minutes.
4. Remove from heat and set aside. Flip each tomato half and brush with olive oil garlic mixture and top with grated parmesan cheese.
5. Close grill and cook for 7-10 minutes more until cheese is melted.
6. Remove tomatoes from the grill and serve immediately.

Just Chicken Satay

 NUTRITION

Calories: 130, Carbs: 9g,

Fat: 8g Protein: 6g

INTOLERANCES:

Gluten-Free, Egg-Free

25 MINUTES   20 MINUTES   20

SHOPPING LIST

- 20 wooden skewers
- 6 eaches boneless, skinless chicken breasts, cut lengthwise into strips
- Marinade:
- 6 tablespoons soy sauce
- 6 tablespoons tomato sauce
- 2 tablespoons peanut oil
- 4 cloves garlic, minced
- 1/2 tsp. ground black pepper
- 1/2 tsp. ground cumin

Peanut Sauce:
- 1 tablespoon peanut oil
- ¼ onion, finely chopped
- 1 clove garlic, minced
- 8 tbsp. peanut butter
- 3 tbsp. white sugar
- 2 tablespoons soy sauce
- 1 cup of water
- 1/2 lemon, juiced

DIRECTIONS

1. If using wooden skewers, put in a deep dish and soak with water, allowing them to soak for 20 minutes.
2. Take a bowl and add the chicken strips and the tomato sauce, peanut oil, soy sauce, cumin, pepper, and garlic and mix well.
3. Ensure the chicken strips are coated well on each side.
4. Marinate for fifteen minutes.
5. After this, add one tablespoon of oil to the warmed skillet over medium to high heat. Add garlic and onion and cook it well. Stir for a few minutes until onion is soft.
6. Now, add soy sauce, butter, water, and sugar and merge well. Cook well

for five minutes, until the sauce gets slowly thickened. Add the juice of a lemon and remove the pan from the flame.
7. Preheat the grill on high heat and lightly oil the grate. Thread every chicken strip on the skewer.
8. Keep the skewers on the preheated grill and cook for ten minutes, flipping through cooking. Serve the satay skewers instantly with peanut sauce.

Easy Grilled Chicken

NUTRITION

Calories: 130,   Carbs: 9g,

Fat: 8g   Protein: 6g

INTOLERANCES:

Gluten-Free, Egg-Free

10 MINUTES

35 MINUTES

12

SHOPPING LIST

- 2 cups white distilled vinegar
- 2 cups of water
- 2 sticks of butter
- 4 tbps. of Worcestershire sauce
- 2 teaspoons minced garlic

- 2 bone-in chicken breasts
- 4 medium chicken leg quarters
- 4 tablespoons garlic salt
- 2 tablespoons ground black pepper
- 1 tablespoon white sugar

DIRECTIONS

1. Mix the Worcestershire sauce, water, vinegar, butter, minced garlic, garlic salt, sugar in a pot and make it boil. After, remove from the flame and allow the marinade to cool at room temperature for 30min.
2. Add the chicken in a plastic bag and pour the marinade over the chicken. Seal the bag and then marinade the chicken for 8hrs or overnight.
3. After, preheat the grill to medium to high heat and lightly oil the grate.
4. Take the chicken from the marinade and add to the grill.
5. Cook the chicken until it gets pink in the middle for 30 - 40 minutes. You can insert a thermometer, (aiming for internal temp of 165F).

Tip: If you are using skinless and boneless chicken breast, lessen the cooking time at eight to ten minutes.

Lemony Chicken in Yogurt

 NUTRITION

Calories: 100, Fat: 8g,
Carbs: 6g, Protein: 1g

 INTOLERANCES

Gluten-Free
Egg-Free

 DIRECTIONS

15 MINUTES

35 MINUTES

6

 **SHOPPING LIST**

- 1/2 cup plain low-fat Greek yogurt
- Half lemon, juiced
- 1 tbsp. lemon zest
- 1 tsp. herbes de Provence
- 1 tsp. salt
- 1 tsp. ground black pepper
- 1 whole chicken, cut into eight pieces
- 1 tbsp. olive oil
- 4 cloves garlic,
- 1 tbsp. paprika
- 1/2 cup plain low-fat Greek yogurt
- 1 tbsp. lemon juice
- 1 tsp. harissa
- A pinch salt

1. First, whisk half juice from olive oil, one teaspoon salt, half cup yogurt, lemon zest, paprika, herbs de Provence, garlic, juice of the half lemon, and black pepper in the bowl. Pour into the plastic bag and then add chicken. Now, coat with marinade and squeeze out the extra air, close the bag. Preserve in the freezer for three hours.
2. Now, preheat the grill for intermediate to high heat and then lightly oil the grate.
3. Mix one tablespoon lemon juice, harissa, half cup yogurt in the little bowl and keep aside.
4. Take out the chicken from the plastic bag and move to the baking sheet lined or plate with paper towels. Now, pat chicken parts dry with more paper towels and then season with a pinch of salt.
5. Now, grill chicken on the preheated grill for at least two minutes and turn every piece and transfer to indirect heat.
6. Grill and turning frequently by using lid until it gets browned and meat gets no longer pink in the middle for thirty to thirty-five minutes.
7. Taking a thermometer and insert in the thickest part of the thigh near the bone. The thermometer should read 165 degrees.
8. Now, serve the chicken with a mixture of yogurt harissa on the side.
9. Additional Tip: Better if served with a side of potatoes or salad.

Chicken Thighs with Salsa

NUTRITION

Calories: 139, Fat: 8g,
Carbs: 4g, Protein: 4g

INTOLERANCES

Gluten-Free
Egg-Free
Lactose-Free

10 MINUTES

30 MINUTES

6

SHOPPING LIST

- ¼ cup extra-virgin olive oil
- 1 orange, juiced
- half tsp. ground cumin
- ¼ tsp. ground coriander
- ¼ tsp. cayenne pepper
- ¼ tsp. smoked paprika
- 1 lime, juiced
- 2 cloves garlic, minced
- 1 pinch salt and ground black pepper
- 8 thighs, bone, and skin removed skinless and boneless chicken thighs
- 1 and a half cups of diced and peeled fresh peaches
- 1 cup pitted and diced red cherries
- ⅓ cup chopped cilantro
- One tablespoon fresh lime juice
- Two tablespoons extra-virgin olive oil
- 2 tbsp. seeded and minced jalapeno pepper
- 2 tbsp. minced red onion

DIRECTIONS

1. Add lime juice, cumin, garlic, paprika, pepper, orange juice, olive oil, garlic, salt, coriander, lime juice and cayenne to the bag. Close and mix the ingredients until mixed well. Add the chicken thighs and press out the excess air and then seal.
2. Place the bag flat in the freezer so that the chicken thighs are in one layer. Allow to marinade for 4 hours and turn the bag over every 2 hours.
3. Prepare the salsa before lighting grill: Mix cherries, cilantro, red onion, peaches, lime juice and jalapeno in a bowl and mix gently . Keep in the freezer for now.
4. Clean and preheat the gas grill to the intermediate heat for twenty minutes.
5. Brush the grill grates with olive oil and then take the chicken thighs from the marinade.
6. Grill the chicken in the one layer until no longer pink in the middle (5 - 7 minutes per side).
7. To check, take a thermometer and insert in the middle of the chicken (it should read at least 165 degrees).
8. Once cooked, serve with salsa.
9. Additional Tip: Peaches should be ripe but not soft.

Lime Chicken Thighs Kebab Style

 NUTRITION

Calories: 100, Fat: 8g,
Carbs: 6g, Protein: 1g

 INTOLERANCES

Gluten-Free
Egg-Free
Lactose-Free

 DIRECTIONS

20 MINUTES

15 MINUTES

4

 **SHOPPING LIST**

Glaze:
- ¼ cup honey
- 1 tbsp. lime juice
- 2 tbsp. Sriracha sauce

Kebabs:
- 8 eaches large metal skewers
- 1 pound boneless and skinless chicken thighs
- Half small fresh pineapples
- 1 medium red onion,
- 1 red sweet pepper
- 1 medium zucchini
- 2 tbsp. olive oil
- one pinch of salt and freshly ground black pepper
- A pinch garlic powder
- A teaspoon lime zest

1. First, preheat the grill to medium to high heat and then lightly oil the grate.
2. Now, whisk lime juice, sriracha sauce, and honey in a little bowl and keep aside. Thread zucchini, red onion, pineapple, chicken, and red pepper on the skewers and put on a plate. Brush with olive oil and season with garlic powder, salt, and pepper.
3. Set the skewers on the warm grate and seal the lid. Reduce the heat to medium. Grill until cooked through (atleast 15 - 20 minutes) turning the skewers every so often.
4. Brush the glaze on both sides of the skewers for two to three minutes and then turn lightly, watching the caramelized glaze. Move to the serving plate and grate lime zest on top, serve hot.
5. Enjoy!

Cilantro Grilled Chicken

 NUTRITION

Calories: 100, Fat: 8g,
Carbs: 6g, Protein: 1g

 INTOLERANCES

Gluten-Free
Egg-Free
Lactose-Free

 DIRECTIONS

15 MINUTES

30 MINUTES

6

 **SHOPPING LIST**

- 4 limes juiced
- Half cup chopped fresh cilantro
- 2 tbsp. of ground black pepper
- 1 whole chicken
- 2 tbsp. garlic salt

1. Take a big ceramic or a big glass bowl and whisk black pepper, lime juice, garlic salt, and cilantro. Now, add the chicken and coat. Wrap the bowl with a plastic cover and preserve it in the freezer for a half-hour, or overnight.
2. Now, preheat the grill to medium to high heat, pour some oil and allow it to get hot.
3. Remove the chicken from the marinade and shake off excess. You can discard the leftover marinade.
4. Cook the chicken on the preheated grill and turn it frequently until it is no longer pink at the bone, (for roughly 30minutes).
5. Take a thermometer and insert near the bone and thermometer should read 165°F.

Chicken Satay Thai Style

 NUTRITION

Calories: 100, Fat: 8g,
Carbs: 6g, Protein: 1g

 INTOLERANCES

Gluten-Free
Egg-Free
Lactose-Free

DIRECTIONS

20 MINUTES

10 MINUTES

8

SHOPPING LIST

- 2 tbsp. vegetable oil
- 2 tbsp. soy sauce
- 1 tsp. ground cumin
- 1 tsp. ground coriander
- 2 pounds skinless, boneless chicken breast
- 20 wooden skewers
- 2 tbsp. of crunchy peanut butter
- 2 tbsp chopped peanuts
- 1 tbsp. lime juice
- 1 tsp. muscovado sugar
- 2 tsp. tamarind paste
- 1 stalk lemongrass
- 2 cloves garlic
- Half tsp. chili powder
- 1 can coconut milk
- 2 tsp. red Thai curry paste
- 1 tbsp. fish sauce
- 1 tbsp. tomato paste
- 1 tbsp. brown sugar

1. Add the lemongrass, soy sauce, tamarind paste, vegetable oil, garlic, muscovado sugar, cumin, chili powder, lime juice, and coriander in a blender to form a smooth paste. Take a plastic bag or a big bowl, toss the chicken strips and marinade. Keep in the freezer for one hour.
2. Now, preheat the grill to medium to high heat, add oil and allow to heat up.
3. Take a little saucepan and merge peanut, fish sauce, brown sugar, curry paste, peanut butter, coconut milk, and tomato paste. Cook it well and stir over middle to low heat until it gets smooth. Keep the sauce warm.
4. Thread the chicken on the skewers. Cook thoroughly, until there is no longer pink in the middle (three to five minutes on every side).
5. Serve with peanut sauce.

Tasty Grilled Chicken

 NUTRITION

Calories: 100, Fat: 8g,
Carbs: 6g, Protein: 1g

 INTOLERANCES

Gluten-Free
Egg-Free
Lactose-Free

 DIRECTIONS

15 MINUTES

1H 30M

6

 SHOPPING LIST

- 1 whole chicken
- 1 pinch salt
- ¼ cup butter, melted
- ¼ tablespoon ground black pepper
- 1 tablespoon salt
- 1 tablespoon paprika

1. First, season the inner side of the chicken with a pinch of salt and put the chicken on to the rotisserie and arrange the grill on high. Cook it well for ten minutes.
2. During this, quickly mix the paprika, 1 tablespoon salt, butter, and pepper and then turn the grill down to intermediate and baste the chicken with this mixture of butter.
3. Seal the lid and cook for one to one and a half hours and then basting infrequently until inner temperature reaches 180°F .
4. Take down the chicken from the rotisserie and allow it t stand for ten to fifteen minutes before slicing into pieces and serve.

Grilled Chicken Marinade

NUTRITION

Calories: 100, Fat: 8g,
Carbs: 6g, Protein: 1g

INTOLERANCES

Gluten-Free
Egg-Free
Lactose-Free

10 MINUTES

15 MINUTES

5

DIRECTIONS

1. First, whisk the olive oil, oregano, soy sauce, parsley, vinegar, garlic powder, basil, and black pepper in a bowl. Now, pour this in a plastic bag. Add the chicken and coat with this marinade. Squeeze out the extra air and close the bag.
2. Marinade in the freezer at least four hours.
3. After this, preheat the grill for middle to low heat and then some oil. Allow this to heat. Take the chicken from the bag, and remove any excess marinade.
4. After, grill the chicken on the preheated grill until there is no longer pink meat (four to five minutes each side). The thermometer should read at least 165 degrees in the middle, when the chicken is ready.

🛒 SHOPPING LIST

- ¼ cup red wine vinegar
- One and a half teaspoons dried parsley flakes
- Half tsp. dried basil
- Half tsp. dried oregano
- ¼ tsp. garlic powder
- ¼ tsp. ground black pepper
- ¼ cup reduced-sodium soy sauce
- ¼ cup olive oil
- 5 pieces of boneless and skinless chicken breasts

Feta Spinach & Turkey Burgers

Calories: 215, Fat: 6g,
Carbs: 9g, Protein: 30g

 INTOLERANCES

Egg-Free

10 MINUTES **10 MINUTES**

 DIRECTIONS

1. Add all ingredients into the mixing bowl and mix until just combined.
2. Make four equal shaped patties from the mixture.
3. Preheat the grill to high heat.
4. Place patties on a hot grill and cook for 3-5 minutes on each side or until internal temperature reaches to 165°F.
5. Serve

SHOPPING LIST

- lb. Ground turkey
- 1 tbsp. Breadcrumbs
- 1/4 tsp. Crushed red pepper
- 1 tsp. Parsley
- 1 tsp. Oregano
- 1 tsp. Garlic powder
- 1/3 cup. Sun-dried tomatoes
- 1/2 cup, crumbled Feta cheese
- 1/2 cup, chopped Baby spinach
- 1/2 tsp. Pepper
- 1/2 tsp. Sea salt

4

Grilled Potato Skewers

 NUTRITION

Calories: 135, Protein: 2g
Fat: 5g, Carbs: 20g

 INTOLERANCES

Gluten-Free
Egg-Free
Lactose-Free

 DIRECTIONS

15 MINUTES

25 MINUTES

4

 **SHOPPING LIST**

- 4 quartered Potatoes
- 1 tsp. Garlic powder
- 2 tsps. Crushed dried rosemary
- 4 tbsps. Dry white wine
- 1/2 cup Mayonnaise
- 1/2 cup Water

1. Add potatoes with water in a microwave-safe bowl and cook in the microwave for 15 minutes or until potatoes are tender.
2. Drain the potatoes and let them cool. In a large mixing bowl, stir together mayonnaise, garlic powder, rosemary, and wine.
3. Add potatoes and mix well.

Cover bowl and place in the refrigerator for 1 hour.
4. Preheat the grill to a high heat and oil grates. Remove potatoes from the marinade and thread onto the skewers.
5. Place potato skewers on a hot grill, cover, and cook for 6-8 minutes. Turn skewers halfway through.
6. Serve.

Curried Cauliflower Skewers

 NUTRITION

Calories: 100, Fat: 8g,
Carbs: 6g, Protein: 1g

 INTOLERANCES

Gluten-Free
Egg-Free
Lactose-Free

 DIRECTIONS

15
MINUTES

15
MINUTES

6

SHOPPING LIST

- 1 cut into florets large cauliflower head
- 1 cut into wedges onion
- 1 cut into squares yellow bell pepper
- 1 fresh lemon juice
- 1/4 cup olive oil
- 1/2 tsp. garlic powder
- 1/2 tsp. ground ginger
- 3 tsps. curry powder
- 1/2 tsp. salt

1. In a large mixing bowl, whisk together oil, lemon juice, garlic, ginger, curry powder, and salt. Add cauliflower florets and toss until well coated.
2. Heat the grill to medium heat.
3. Thread cauliflower florets, onion, and bell pepper onto the skewers.
4. Place skewers onto the hot grill and cook for 6-7 minutes on each side.
5. Serve.

Southwest Chicken Drumsticks

 NUTRITION

Calories: 100, Fat: 8g,
Carbs: 6g, Protein: 1g

 INTOLERANCES

Gluten-Free
Egg-Free
Lactose-Free

 10 MINUTES

 **30 MINUTES**

 **SHOPPING LIST**

- 2 lbs. Chicken legs
- 2 tbsps. Taco seasoning
- 2 tbsps. Olive oil

 DIRECTIONS

1. Preheat the grill to a medium-high heat and oil grates.
2. Brush chicken legs with oil and rub with taco seasoning.
3. Place chicken legs on the hot grill and cook for 30 minutes.
4. Turn chicken legs after every 10 minutes.
5. Serve.

 **4**

Sweet Potato Fries

 NUTRITION

Calories: 230, Fat: 6g,
Carbs: 40g, Protein: 4g

 INTOLERANCES

Gluten-Free
Egg-Free
Lactose-Free

 DIRECTIONS

1. Preheat the grill to medium-high heat.
2. Toss sweet potatoes with oil, pepper, and salt.
3. Place sweet potato wedges on a hot grill and cook over a medium heat for 6 minutes.
4. Flip and cook for 6-8 minutes more.
5. Serve.

10 MINUTES

12 MINUTES

4

SHOPPING LIST

- 2 lbs. peeled and cut into ½-inch wedges Sweet potatoes
- 2 tbsps. Olive oil
- Pepper and salt to taste

Balsamic Mushroom Skewers

 NUTRITION

Calories: 60, Fat: 1g,
Carbs: 8g, Protein: 6g

 INTOLERANCES

Gluten-Free
Egg-Free
Lactose-Free

 DIRECTIONS

10 MINUTES

10 MINUTES

SHOPPING LIST

- 2 lbs. sliced ¼-inch thick Mushrooms
- 1/2 tsp. chopped Thyme
- 3 chopped Garlic cloves
- 1 tbsp. Soy sauce
- 2 tbsps. Balsamic vinegar
- Pepper and salt to taste

1. Add mushrooms and remaining ingredients into the mixing bowl, cover, and place in the refrigerator for 30 minutes.
2. Thread marinated mushrooms onto the skewers.
3. Heat the grill to medium-high heat. Place mushroom skewers onto the hot grill and cook for 2-3 minutes per side.
4. Serve.

4

CHAPTER 4

Beef Recipes

Asian Soy Marinated Steak

 NUTRITION

Calories: 300, Fat: 20g,
Carbs: 8g, Protein: 22g

 INTOLERANCES

Gluten-Free
Egg-Free
Lactose-Free

 DIRECTIONS

20 MINUTES

20 MINUTES

SHOPPING LIST

- 1/2 chopped onion
- 3 chopped cloves of garlic
- 1/4 cup of olive oil
- 1/4 cup of balsamic vinegar
- 1/4 cup of soy sauce
- 1 tablespoon of Dijon mustard
- 1 tablespoon of rosemary
- 1 teaspoon of salt to taste
- 1/2 teaspoon of ground black pepper to taste
- 1 1/2 pounds of flank steak

1. Using a large mixing bowl, add in all the ingredients on the list aside from the steak then mix properly to combine.
2. Place the steak in a Ziploc bag, pour in the prepared marinade then shake properly to coat.
3. Place the bag in the refrigerator and let the steak marinate for about thirty minutes to two full days.
4. Preheat the Wood Pellet Smoker and Grill to 350-400°F, remove the steak from its marinade then set the marinade aside for blasting.
5. Place the steak on the preheated grill then grill for about six to eight minutes until the beef is heated through.
6. Flip the steak over and cook for an additional six minutes until an inserted thermometer reads 150°F.
7. Place the steak on a cutting board and let rest for about five minutes. Slice and serve.

4

Grilled Steak and Vegetable Kebabs

5

 NUTRITION

Calories: 350, Fat: 14g,
Carbs: 18g, Protein: 34g

 INTOLERANCES

Gluten-Free
Egg-Free
Lactose-Free

15 MINUTES

20 MINUTES

 DIRECTIONS

1. Using a large mixing bowl, add in the oil, soy sauce, lemon juice, red wine vinegar, Worcestershire sauce, Dijon, honey, garlic, and pepper to taste then mix properly to combine.
2. Using a sharp knife, cut the steak into smaller pieces or cubes then add to a resealable bag.
3. Pour the marinade into the bag with steak then shake to coat. Let the steak marinate for about three to six hours in the refrigerator.
4. Preheat the Wood Pellet Smoker and Grill to 425°F, place the veggies into a mixing bowl, add in oil, garlic powder, salt, and pepper to taste then mix to combine.
5. Thread the veggies and steak alternately unto skewers, place the skewers on the preheated grill and grill for about eight to nine minutes until it is cooked through.
6. Make sure you turn the kebabs occasionally as you cook.
7. Serve.

 **SHOPPING LIST**

Marinade
- 1/4 cup of olive oil
- 1/4 cup of soy sauce
- 1 1/2 tablespoons of fresh lemon juice
- 1 1/2 tablespoons of red wine vinegar
- 2 1/2 tablespoons of Worcestershire sauce
- 1 tablespoon of honey
- 2 teaspoons of Dijon mustard
- 1 tablespoon of garlic
- 1 teaspoon of freshly ground black pepper to taste

Kebabs
- 1 3/4 lbs. of sirloin steak
- 1 sliced zucchini.
- 3 sliced bell peppers
- 1 large and sliced red onion
- 1 tablespoon of olive oil
- Salt and freshly ground black pepper to taste
- 1/2 teaspoon of garlic powder

Barbecue Beef Ribs on the grill

NUTRITION

Calories: 280,   94mg,

Fat: 42g,   Carbs: 6g

Cholesterol: Protein: 55g

INTOLERANCES

Gluten-Free
Egg-Free
Lactose-Free

30 MINUTES

4

1 HOUR

DIRECTIONS

 **SHOPPING LIST**

- 1/2 cup of Dijon mustard
- 2 tablespoons of cider vinegar
- 3 lbs. of spareribs
- 4 tablespoons of paprika powder
- 1/2 tablespoon of chili powder
- 1 1/2 tablespoon of garlic powder
- 2 teaspoons of ground cumin
- 2 teaspoon of onion powder
- 1 1/2 tablespoon of ground black pepper to taste
- 2 tablespoons of salt to taste
- 2 tablespoons of butter, which is optional

1. Preheat a Wood Pellet Smoker and Grill to 350°F, using a small mixing bowl, add in the mustard and the vinegar then mix properly to combine.
2. Rub the mixture on the spareribs, coating all sides. Using another mixing bowl, add the paprika powder, chili powder, garlic powder, cumin, onion powder, salt, and pepper to taste then mix properly to combine.
3. Reserve a small quantity of the mixture, seasoned the spareribs with the rest of the spice mixture, coating all sides.
4. Wrap the seasoned ribs in aluminum foil, top with the butter if desired then place the ribs on the preheated grill.

5. Grill the ribs for about one hour until it is cooked through. Make sure you flip after every twenty minutes.
6. Once the ribs are cooked through, remove from the grill, unwrap the aluminum foil then grill the ribs for another two to five minutes until crispy.
7. Let the ribs cool for a few minutes, slice, and serve.

Garlic Butter Grilled Steak

 NUTRITION

Calories: 543, Fat: 25g,
Carbs: 1g, Protein: 64g

 INTOLERANCES

Gluten-Free
Egg-Free
Lactose-Free

 DIRECTIONS

15 MINUTES

4

20 MINUTES

SHOPPING LIST

- 3 tablespoons of unsalted butter
- 4 cloves of garlic
- 1 tablespoon of chopped parsley
- 1 tablespoon of olive oil
- 4 strip steaks
- Salt and pepper to taste

1. Using a large mixing bowl, add in the butter, garlic, and parsley then mix properly to combine, set aside in the refrigerator.
2. Preheat a Wood Pellet Smoker and Grill to 400° F, use paper towels to pat the steak dry, rub oil on all sides then season with some sprinkles of salt and pepper to taste.
3. Place the seasoned steak on the preheated grill and grill for about four to five minutes.
4. Flip the steak over and grill for an additional four to five minutes until it becomes brown in color and cooked as desired.
5. Rub the steak with the butter mixture, heat on the grill for a few minutes, slice, and serve.

Grilled Herb Steak

NUTRITION

Calories: 440, Fat: 25g,
Cholesterol: 90mg, Carbs: 20g, Protein: 35g

INTOLERANCES

Gluten-Free
Egg-Free
Lactose-Free

20 MINUTES

DIRECTIONS

1. Using a grinder or a food processor, add in the peppercorns and the fennel seeds then blend until completely crushed then add to a mixing bowl.
2. Add in the garlic, rosemary, thyme, salt, and pepper to taste then mix properly to combine, set aside.
3. Rub the steak with oil, coating all sides then coat with half of the peppercorn mixture. Make sure the steak is coated all round.
4. Place the steak in a Ziploc plastic bag then let marinate in the refrigerator for about 2 to 8 minutes.
5. Preheat a Wood Pellet Smoker and Grill to 450°F, place the coated steak on the grill and cook for about five to six minutes.
6. Flip the steak over and cook for another five to six minutes until cooked through.
7. Once cooked, let the steak cool for a few minutes, slice, and serve.

SHOPPING LIST

- 1 tablespoon of peppercorns
- 1 teaspoon of fennel seeds
- 3 large and minced cloves of garlic
- 2 teaspoons of kosher salt to taste
- 1 tablespoon of chopped rosemary
- 1 tablespoon of chopped thyme
- 2 teaspoons of black pepper to taste
- 2 teaspoons of olive oil
- 1 pound of flank steak

4

15 MINUTES

BBQ Meatloaf

25 MINUTES

1hr 30 MINUTES

SHOPPING LIST

- 1 1/2 pounds of ground beef
- 1/3 cup of ketchup
- 2 teaspoons of Worcestershire sauce
- 1 large egg
- 1 cup of soft breadcrumbs
- 1 cup of chopped onions
- 1/2 teaspoon of salt to taste
- 1/4 teaspoon of ground black pepper to taste
- Barbecue sauce for a glaze

NUTRITION

Calories: 370, Fat: 15g, Carbs: 20g, Protein: 35g

INTOLERANCES

Lactose-Free

4

DIRECTIONS

1. Preheat a Wood Pellet Smoker and Grill to 350°F, using a large mixing bowl, add in the beef alongside with the rest of the ingredients on the list (aside from the barbecue sauce) them mix properly to combine.
2. Place the beef mixture in an aluminum foil then form into your desired loaf shape.
3. Unfold the foil, brush the meatloaf with barbecue sauce then warp in.
4. Place the meatloaf on the grill and cook for about 1 hour to 1 hour and 30 minutes until it attains a temperature of 160°F.
5. Slice and serve.

Unconventional Cocoa Rub Steak

 NUTRITION

Calories: 480, Fat: 30g,
Carbs: 4g, Protein: 40g

 INTOLERANCES

Gluten-Free
Egg-Free
Lactose-Free

 DIRECTIONS

1. Mix in a bowl, the cocoa powder, brown sugar, paprika, garlic powder, onion powder, and salt to taste. Mix well.
2. Rub the steak with about two tablespoons of the spice mixture, coating all sides then let rest for a few minutes.
3. Preheat the Wood Pellet Smoker and Grill to 450°F, place the steak on the grill, and grill for a few minutes on both sides until it is cooked as desired.
4. Once cooked, cover the steak in a foil and let rest for a few minutes, serve and enjoy.

10 MINUTES

10 MINUTES

4

 **SHOPPING LIST**

- 4 ribeye steaks
- 2 tablespoons of unsweetened cocoa powder
- 1 tablespoon of dark brown sugar
- 1 tablespoon of smoked paprika
- 1 teaspoon of sea salt to taste
- 1 teaspoon of black pepper
- 1/2 teaspoon of garlic powder
- 1/2 teaspoon of onion powder

Grilled Steak with a Mushroom Sauce

25 MINUTES

1hr 30 MINUTES

4

 **SHOPPING LIST**

- 1/2 cup of Dijon mustard
- 2 minced cloves of garlic
- 2 tablespoons of bourbon
- 1 tablespoon of Worcestershire sauce
- 4 beefsteak tenderloin
- 1 tbsp. of peppercorns
- 1 tbsp. of extra-virgin olive oil
- 1 small and diced onion
- 1 minced clove of garlic
- 1/2 cup of white wine
- 1/2 cup of chicken stock
- 16 ounces of sliced mushrooms
- 1/2 cup of heavy cream
- Salt and pepper to taste

 DIRECTIONS

1. Using a small mixing bowl, add in the mustard, garlic, bourbon, and Worcestershire sauce then mix properly to combine
2. Place the steak in a Ziploc back, pour in the mustard mixture then shake properly to coat. Let the steak sit for about sixty minutes.
3. Using a small mixing bowl, add in the peppercorns, salt, and pepper to taste then mix to combine.
4. Remove the steak from the Ziploc bag, season the steak with the peppercorn mixture then use clean hands to evenly distribute the seasoning.
5. Preheat the Wood Pellet Smoker and grill to 180°F then close the lid for fifteen minutes.
6. Add the seasoned steak on the grill and smoke for about sixty minutes. Take the steak out of the grill, increase the temperature of the grill to 350 degrees and grill for 20 to 30 minutes until it attains an internal temperature of 130°F.
7. To make the sauce, place a pan on the griddle, add in oil and onions then cook for a few minutes.
8. Cook the garlic for one minute. Add in the mushrooms and cook for a few more minutes.
9. Add in the stock, wine, salt, and pepper to taste, stir to combine then bring to a simmer. Simmer the sauce for 5 to 7 minutes then add in the heavy cream.
10. Stir to combine then serve the steak with the sauce, enjoy.

Tender Beef

 NUTRITION

Calories: 425, Fat: 21g,
Cholesterol: 170mg, Protein: 55g

 INTOLERANCES

Gluten-Free
Egg-Free
Lactose-Free

10 MINUTES

1hr 20 MINUTES

4

SHOPPING LIST

- 1 (5-pound) beef tenderloin, trimmed
- Kosher salt, as required
- ¼ cup olive oil
- Freshly ground black pepper, as required

 DIRECTIONS

1. With kitchen strings, tie the tenderloin at 7-8 places.
2. Season tenderloin with kosher salt generously.
3. With a plastic wrap, cover the tenderloin and keep aside at room temperature for about 1 hour.
4. Preheat the Wood Pellet Grill & Smoker on grill setting to 225-250°F.
5. Coat tenderloin with oil evenly and season with black pepper.
6. Arrange tenderloin onto the grill and cook for about 55-65 minutes.
7. Place cooking grate directly over hot coals and sear tenderloin for about 2 minutes per side.
8. Remove the tenderloin from the grill and place onto a cutting board for about 10-15 minutes before serving.
9. With a sharp knife, cut the tenderloin into desired-sized slices and serve.

Mustard Beef Short Ribs

 NUTRITION

Calories: 867, Fat: 37g,
Cholesterol: 361 mg, Carbs: 7 g,
Protein: 117g

INTOLERANCES:

Gluten-Free
Egg-Free
Lactose-Free

 6

 15 MINUTES

 2 HOURS

 SHOPPING LIST

For Mustard Sauce:
- 1 cup prepared yellow mustard
- 1/4 cup red wine vinegar
- 1/4 cup dill pickle juice
- 2 tablespoons soy sauce
- 2 tablespoons Worcestershire sauce
- 1 teaspoon ground ginger
- 1 teaspoon granulated garlic

For Spice Rub:
- 2 tablespoons salt
- 2 tablespoons freshly ground black pepper
- 1 tablespoon white cane sugar
- 1 tablespoon granulated garlic

For Ribs :
- 6 (14-ounce) (4-5-inch long) beef short ribs

 DIRECTIONS

1. Preheat the Wood Pellet Grill & Smoker on smoke setting to 230-250°F, using charcoal.

For the Sauce:

2. In a bowl, mix together all ingredients.

For Rub:

3. In a small bowl, mix together all ingredients.

4. Coat the ribs with sauce generously and then sprinkle with spice rub evenly.

5. Place the ribs onto the grill over indirect heat, bone side down. Cook for about 1-1½ hours.

6. Flip the side and cook for about 45

minutes. Repeat.

7. Remove the ribs from grill and place onto a cutting board for about 10 minutes before serving.

8. With a sharp knife, cut the ribs into equal sized individual pieces and serve.

Sweet and Spicy Beef Brisket

NUTRITION

Calories: 536, Fat: 15g, Cholesterol: 203 mg, Carbs: 24g, Protein: 71g

INTOLERANCES:

Gluten-Free
Egg-Free
Lactose-Free

10 MINUTES

SHOPPING LIST

- 1 cup paprika
- 3/4 cup sugar
- 3 tablespoons garlic salt
- 3 tablespoons onion powder
- 1 tablespoon celery salt
- 1 tablespoon lemon pepper
- 1 tablespoon ground black pepper
- 1 teaspoon cayenne pepper
- 1 teaspoon mustard powder
- 1/2 teaspoon dried thyme, crushed
- 1 (5-6-pound) beef brisket, trimmed

DIRECTIONS

10

7 HOURS

1. In a bowl, place all ingredients except for beef brisket and mix well.
2. Rub the brisket with spice mixture generously.
3. With a plastic wrap, cover the brisket and refrigerate overnight.
4. Preheat the Z Grills Wood Pellet Grill & Smoker on grill setting to 250°F.
5. Place the brisket onto grill over indirect heat and cook for about 3-3½ hours.
6. Flip and cook for about 3-3½ hours more.
7. Remove the brisket from grill and place onto a cutting board for about 10-15 minutes before slicing.
8. With a sharp knife, cut the brisket in desired sized slices and serve.

Beef Rump Roast

NUTRITION

Calories: 252, Fat: 9 g,
Cholesterol: 113mg, Carbs: 2g,
Protein: 37g

INTOLERANCES:

Gluten-Free
Egg-Free
Lactose-Free

10 MINUTES

8

6 HOURS

SHOPPING LIST

- 1 teaspoon smoked paprika
- 1 teaspoon cayenne pepper
- 1 teaspoon onion powder
- 1 teaspoon garlic powder
- Salt and ground black pepper, as required
- 3 pounds beef rump roast
- 1/4 cup Worcestershire sauce

DIRECTIONS

1. Preheat the Wood Pellet Grill & Smoker on smoke setting to 200°F, using charcoal.
2. In a bowl, mix together all spices.
3. Coat the rump roast with Worcestershire sauce evenly and then, rub with spice mixture generously.
4. Place the rump roast onto the grill and cook for about 5-6 hours.
5. Remove the roast from the grill and place onto a cutting board for about 10-15 minutes before serving.
6. With a sharp knife, cut the roast into desired-sized slices and serve.

Spicy Chuck Roast

10 MINUTES

3 HOURS

8

NUTRITION

Calories: 645, Fat: 48 g,
Cholesterol: 175 mg, Carbs: 4g,
Protein: 46g

INTOLERANCES:

Gluten-Free
Egg-Free
Lactose-Free

SHOPPING LIST

- 2 tablespoons onion powder
- 2 tablespoons garlic powder
- 1 tablespoon red chili powder
- 1 tablespoon cayenne pepper
- Salt and ground black pepper, as required
- 1 (3 pound) beef chuck roast
- 16 fluid ounces warm beef broth

DIRECTIONS

1. Preheat the grill setting to 250°F.
2. In a bowl, mix together spices, salt and black pepper.
3. Rub the chuck roast with spice mixture evenly.
4. Place the rump roast onto the grill and cook for about 1½ hours per side.
5. Arrange chuck roast in a steaming pan with beef broth.
6. With a piece of foil, cover the pan and cook for about 2-3 hours.
7. Remove the chuck roast from grill and place onto a cutting board for about 20 minutes before slicing.
8. With a sharp knife, cut the chuck roast into desired-sized slices and serve.

BBQ Spiced Flank Steak

NUTRITION

Calories: 370, Fat: 19g
Cholesterol: 148mg, Carbs: 1g,
Protein: 46g

INTOLERANCES:

Gluten-Free
Egg-Free

15 MINUTES

30 MINUTES

6

SHOPPING LIST

- 1 (2-pound) beef flank steak
- 2 tablespoons olive oil
- 1/4 cup BBQ rub
- 3 tablespoons blue cheese, crumbled
- 2 tablespoons butter,
- softened
- 1 teaspoon fresh chive, minced

DIRECTIONS

1. Preheat the grill setting to 225°F.
2. Coat the steak with oil evenly and season with BBQ rub.
3. Place the steak onto the grill and cook for about 10-15 minutes per side.
4. Remove the steak from grill and place onto a cutting board for about 10 minutes before slicing.
5. In a bowl, add blue cheese, butter and chives and mix well.
6. With a sharp knife, cut the steak into thin strips across the grain.
7. Top with cheese mixture and serve.

Roasted Whole Ham in Apricot Sauce

NUTRITION

Calories: 675, Fat: 14g,
Cholesterol: 93 mg, Carbs: 90g,
Protein: 43g

INTOLERANCES:

Gluten-Free
Egg-Free

15
MINUTES

SHOPPING LIST

- 8-pound whole ham, bone-in
- 16 ounces apricot BBQ sauce
- 2 tablespoon Dijon mustard
- 1/4 cup horseradish

2
HOURS

8

DIRECTIONS

1. Switch on the grill, fill the grill hopper with apple-flavored wood pellets, power the grill on by using the control panel, select 'smoke' on the temperature dial, or set the temperature to 325 degrees F and let it preheat for a minimum of 15 minutes.
2. Meanwhile, take a large roasting pan, line it with foil, and place ham on it.
3. When the grill has preheated, open the lid, place roasting pan containing ham on the grill grate, shut the grill and smoke for 1 hour and 30 minutes.
4. Meanwhile, prepare the glaze and for this, take a medium saucepan, place it over medium heat, add BBQ sauce, mustard, and horseradish, stir until mixed and cook for 5 minutes, set aside until required.
5. After 1 hour and 30 minutes smoking, brush ha generously with the prepared glaze and continue smoking for 30 minutes until internal temperature reaches 135 degrees F.
6. When done, remove roasting pan from the grill, let rest for 20 minutes and then cut into slices.
7. Serve ham with remaining glaze.

Beef Stuffed Bell Peppers

20 MINUTES

1 HOURS

6

SHOPPING LIST

- 6 large bell peppers
- 1-pound ground beef
- 1 small onion, chopped
- 2 garlic cloves, minced
- 2 cups cooked rice
- 1 cup frozen corn, thawed
- 1 cup cooked black beans
- 2/3 cup salsa
- 2 tablespoons Cajun rub
- 1 ½ cups Monterey Jack cheese, grated

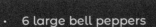
DIRECTIONS

1. Cut each bell pepper in half lengthwise through the stem. Carefully, remove the seeds and ribs.

For stuffing:

2. Heat a large frying pan and cook the beef for about 6-7 minutes or until browned completely.
3. Add onion and garlic and cook for about 2-3 minutes.
4. Stir in remaining ingredients except cheese and cook for about 5 minutes.
5. Remove from the heat and set aside to cool slightly.
6. Preheat the grill setting to 350°F.
7. Stuff each bell pepper half with stuffing mixture evenly.
8. Arrange the peppers onto grill, stuffing side up and cook for about 40 minutes.
9. Sprinkle each bell pepper half with cheese and cook for about 5 minutes more.
10. Remove the bell peppers from grill and serve hot.

Brandy Beef

📖 NUTRITION

Calories: 496, Fat: 29g,
Cholesterol: 180 mg, Carbs: 4g,
Protein: 44g

📖 INTOLERANCES:

Gluten-Free
Egg-Free

140 MINUTES

15 MINUTES

6

🧺 SHOPPING LIST

- For Brandy Butter:
- 1/2 cup butter
- 1-ounce brandy

For Brandy Sauce:
- 2 ounces brandy
- 8 garlic cloves, minced
- 1/4 cup mixed fresh

herbs (parsley, rosemary and thyme), chopped
- 2 teaspoons honey
- 2 teaspoons hot English mustard

For Tenderloin:
- 1 (2-pound) center-cut beef tenderloin
- Salt and cracked black peppercorns, as required

📖 DIRECTIONS

1. Preheat the grill setting to 230° F.
2. For brandy butter:
3. In a pan, melt butter over medium-low heat.
4. Stir in brandy and remove from heat. Set aside, covered to keep warm.

For brandy Sauce:

5. In a bowl, add all ingredients and mix until well combined.
6. Season the tenderloin with salt and black peppercorns generously.
7. Coat tenderloin with brandy sauce evenly.
8. With a baster-injector, inject tenderloin with brandy butter.
9. Place the tenderloin onto the grill and cook for about ½-2 hours, injecting with brandy butter occasionally.
10. Remove the tenderloin from grill and place onto a cutting board for about 10-15 minutes before serving.
11. With a sharp knife, cut the tenderloin into desired-sized slices and serve.

CHAPTER 5

Lamb
Recipes

Smoked Lamb Shoulder

15 MINUTES

1 HR 30 MINUTES

4

NUTRITION
Calories: 240, Fat: 19g, Protein: 17g

INTOLERANCES:
Gluten-Free
Egg-Free
Lactose-Free

SHOPPING LIST

- For Smoked Lamb Shoulder
- 5 lb. lamb shoulder, boneless and excess fat trimmed
- 2 tbsp kosher salt
- 2 tbsp black pepper
- 1 tbsp rosemary, dried
- The Injection
- 1 cup apple cider vinegar
- The Spritz
- 1 cup apple cider vinegar
- 1 cup apple juice

DIRECTIONS

1. Preheat the wood pellet smoker with a water pan to 2250°F.
2. Rinse the lamb in cold water then pat it dry with a paper towel. Inject vinegar to the lamb.
3. Dry the lamb again and rub with oil, salt black pepper and rosemary. Tie with kitchen twine.
4. Smoke uncovered for 1 hour then spritz after every 15 minutes until the internal temperature reaches 1950°F.
5. Remove the lamb from the grill and place it on a platter. Let cool before shredding it and enjoying it with your favorite side.

Smoked
Pulled Lamb Sliders

 NUTRITION

Calories: 339, Fat: 22g,
Carbs: 16g, Protein: 18g

 **INTOLERANCES:**

Egg-Free
Lactose-Free

SHOPPING LIST

10 MINUTES

7 HOURS

7

- 5 lb. lamb shoulder, boneless
- 1/2 cup olive oil
- 1/4 cup dry rub
- 10 oz spritz
- The Dry Rub
- 1/3 cup kosher salt
- 1/3 cup pepper, ground
- 1-1/3 cup garlic, granulated
- The Spritz
- 4 oz Worcestershire sauce
- 6 oz apple cider vinegar

 **DIRECTIONS**

1. Preheat the wood pellet smoker with a water bath to 250°F.
2. Trim any fat from the lamb then rub with oil and dry rub.
3. Place the lamb on the smoker for 90 minutes then spritz with a spray bottle every 30 minutes until the internal temperature reaches 165°F.
4. Transfer the lamb shoulder to a foil pan with the remaining spritz liquid and cover tightly with foil.
5. Place back in the smoker and smoke until the internal temperature reaches 200°F.
6. Remove from the smoker and let rest for 30 minutes before pulling the lamb and serving with slaw, bun, or aioli.
7. Enjoy!

Smoked Lamb Meatballs

 NUTRITION

Calories: 73, Fat: 5g,
Carbs: 2g, Protein: 5g

 INTOLERANCES

Egg-Free
Lactose-Free

5

10
MINUTES

1
Hour

 DIRECTIONS

1. Set the wood pellet smoker to 250°F using a fruitwood.
2. In a mixing bowl, combine all meatball ingredients until well mixed.
3. Form small-sized balls and place them on a baking sheet. Place the baking sheet in the smoker and smoke until the internal temperature reaches 160°F.
4. Remove from the smoker and serve.
5. Enjoy.

 **SHOPPING LIST**

- 1 lb. lamb shoulder, ground
- 3 garlic cloves, finely diced
- 3 tbsp shallot, diced
- 1 tbsp salt
- 1 egg
- 1/2 tbsp pepper
- 1/2 tbsp cumin
- 1/2 tbsp smoked paprika
- 1/4 tbsp red pepper flakes
- 1/4 tbsp cinnamon, ground
- 1/4 cup panko breadcrumbs

Crown Rack of Lamb

NUTRITION

Calories: 390, Fat: 35g,
Protein: 17g

INTOLERANCES

Gluten-Free

Egg-Free

Lactose-Free

DIRECTIONS

SHOPPING LIST

- 2 racks of lamb, frenched
- 1 tbsp garlic, crushed
- 1 tbsp rosemary, finely chopped
- 1/4 cup olive oil
- 2 feet twine

10 MINUTES

30 MINUTES

6

1. Rinse the racks with cold water then pat them dry with a paper towel.
2. Lay the racks on a flat board then score between each bone, about ¼ inch down.
3. In a mixing bowl, mix garlic, rosemary, and oil then generously brush on the lamb.
4. Take each lamb rack and bend it into a semicircle forming a crown-like shape.
5. Use the twine to wrap the racks about 4 times starting from the base to the top. Make sure you tie the twine tightly to keep the racks together.
6. Preheat the wood pellet to 400-450°F then place the lamb racks on a baking dish.
7. Cook for 10 minutes then reduce temperature to 300°F. cook for 20 more minutes or until the internal temperature reaches 130°F.
8. Remove the lamb rack from the wood pellet and let rest for 15 minutes.
9. Serve when hot with veggies and potatoes.
10. Bon Appetit!

Smoking Leg of Lamb

 NUTRITION

Calories: 350, Fat: 16g,
Carbs: 3g, Protein: 49g

 INTOLERANCES

Gluten-Free
Egg-Free
Lactose-Free

 DIRECTIONS

15 MINUTES

3 Hour

6

SHOPPING LIST

- 1 leg lamb, boneless
- 4 garlic cloves, minced
- 2 tbsp salt
- 1 tbsp black pepper, freshly ground
- 2 tbsp oregano
- 1 tbsp thyme
- 2 tbsp olive oil

1. Trim any excess fat from the lamb and tie the lamb using twine to form a nice roast.
2. In a mixing bowl, mix garlic, spices, and oil. Rub all over the lamb, wrap with a plastic bag then refrigerate for an hour to marinate.
3. Place the lamb on a smoker set at 250°F. smoke the lamb for 4 hours or until the internal temperature reaches 1450°F.
4. Remove from the smoker and let rest to cool. Serve and enjoy.

Traditional Grilled Lamb Chops

 NUTRITION

Calories: 519, Fat: 45g,
Carbs: 2g, Protein: 25g

 INTOLERANCES

Gluten-Free
Egg-Free
Lactose-Free

 DIRECTIONS

10 MINUTES

15 MINUTES

6

SHOPPING LIST

- 1/4 cup distilled white vinegar
- 2 tbsp salt
- 1/2 tbsp black pepper
- 1 tbsp garlic, minced
- 1 onion, thinly sliced
- 2 tbsp olive oil
- 2 lb. lamb chops

1. In a resealable bag, mix vinegar, salt, black pepper, garlic, sliced onion, and oil until all salt has dissolved.
2. Add the lamb chops and toss until well coated. Place in the fridge to marinate for 2 hours.
3. Preheat the wood pellet grill to high heat.
4. Remove the lamb from the fridge and discard the marinade. Wrap any exposed bones with foil.
5. Grill the lamb for 3 minutes per side. You can also broil in a broiler for more crispness.
6. Serve and enjoy.

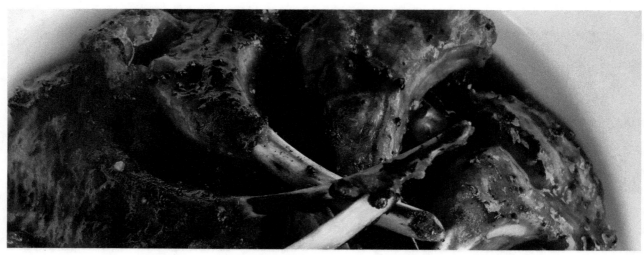

Spicy Chinese Cumin Lamb Skewers

NUTRITION

Calories: 77, Fat: 5g,
Carbs: 2g, Protein: 6g

INTOLERANCES

Gluten-Free
Egg-Free
Lactose-Free

DIRECTIONS

20 MINUTES

10 MINUTES

10

SHOPPING LIST

- 1 lb. lamb shoulder, cut into 1/2-inch pieces
- 10 skewers
- 2 tbsp ground cumin
- 2 tbsp red pepper flakes
- 1 tbsp salt

1. Thread the lamb pieces onto skewers.
2. Preheat the wood pellet grill to medium heat and lightly oil the grill grate.
3. Place the skewers on the grill grate and cook while turning occasionally. Sprinkle cumin, pepper flakes, and salt every time you turn the skewer.
4. Cook for 6 minutes or until nicely browned.
5. Serve and enjoy.

Garlic and Rosemary Lamb Chops on the grill

NUTRITION

Calories: 171, Fat: 8g,
Carbs: 1g, Protein: 23g

INTOLERANCES

Gluten-Free
Egg-Free
Lactose-Free

DIRECTIONS

1. In a small mixing bowl, mix garlic, lemon zest, oil, salt, and black pepper then pour the mixture over the lamb.
2. Flip the lamb chops to make sure they are evenly coated. Place the chops in the fridge to marinate for an hour.
3. Preheat the wood pellet grill to high heat then sear the lamb for 3 minutes on each side.
4. Reduce the heat and cook the chops for 6 minutes or until the internal temperature reaches 150°F.
5. Remove the lamb from the grill and wrap it in a foil.
6. Let it rest for 5 minutes before serving.
7. Enjoy!

4

20 MINUTES

10 MINUTES

SHOPPING LIST

- 2 lb. lamb loin, thick cut
- 4 garlic cloves, minced
- 1 tbsp rosemary leaves, fresh chopped
- 1 tbsp kosher salt
- 1/2 tbsp black pepper
- 1 lemon zest
- 1/4 cup olive oil

Lamb's Leg Traditional Steaks

 NUTRITION

Calories: 325, Fat: 22g,
Carbs: 2g, Protein: 30g

 INTOLERANCES

Gluten-Free
Egg-Free
Lactose-Free

 DIRECTIONS

1. Place the lamb in a shallow dish in a single layer. Top with oil, garlic cloves, rosemary, salt, and black pepper then flip the steaks to cover on both sides.
2. Let sit for 30 minutes to marinate.
3. Preheat the wood pellet grill to high and brush the grill grate with oil.
4. Place the lamb steaks on the grill grate and cook until browned and the internal is slightly pink. The internal temperature should be 140°F.
5. Let rest for 5 minutes before serving.
6. Enjoy.

10 MINUTES

10 MINUTES

4

 **SHOPPING LIST**

- 4 lamb steaks, bone-in
- 1/4 cup olive oil
- 4 garlic cloves, minced
- 1 tbsp rosemary, freshly chopped
- Salt and black pepper

Lamb Loin Chops

 NUTRITION

Calories: 570, Fat: 44g,
Carbs: 1g, Protein: 42g

 INTOLERANCES

Gluten-Free
Egg-Free
Lactose-Free

10 MINUTES

10 MINUTES

 **SHOPPING LIST**

- 2 tbsp herbs de Provence
- 1-1/2 tbsp olive oil
- 2 garlic cloves, minced
- 2 tbsp lemon juice
- 5 oz lamb loin chops
- Salt and black pepper to taste

 DIRECTIONS

1. In a small mixing bowl, mix herbs de Provence, oil, garlic, and juice. Rub the mixture on the lamb chops then refrigerate for an hour.
2. Preheat the wood pellet grill to medium-high then lightly oil the grill grate.
3. Season the lamb chops with salt and black pepper.
4. Place the lamb chops on the grill and cook for 4 minutes on each side.
5. Remove the chops from the grill and place them in an aluminum covered plate. Let rest for 5 minutes before serving.

6

Smoked Lamb Shoulder Sausage

 **NUTRITION**

Calories: 190, Fat: 16g,
Carbohydrates: 3g, Protein: 17g

15 MINUTES

1 hr 20 MINUTES

7

INTOLERANCES

Gluten-Free
Egg-Free
Lactose-Free

DIRECTIONS

1. Start by cutting the lamb shoulder into pieces of 2 inches peach and grind the meat with the help of a meat grinder.
2. Combine the lamb with all the spices in a large bowl and let refrigerate with the spices for several hours.
3. With a sausage horn; attach the hog casing; then start to feed the sausage through the grinder to fill the casing and twist it into links.
4. With a knife, prick some holes along the casing and refrigerate for about 30 minutes.
5. Combine all your ingredients to make the yogurt sauce in a medium bowl. Cover the yogurt sauce and refrigerate.
6. Start your Wood Pellet Smoker or grill on smoke and let the lid open until a fire is established for about 4 minutes.
7. Set the temperature to about 225°F and place the sausage on the grill grate and let smoke for about 1 hour.
8. Once the time is up, remove the lamb links from the grill and turn the temperature to High and place the lamb links back on the grill and cook for about 5 minutes per side.
9. Serve your lamb sausages with yogurt and roasted veggies or potatoes.
10. Enjoy your delicious dish!

SHOPPING LIST

- Ingredients:
- 2 Pounds of lamb shoulder
- 60 Inches of hog casing
- 1 tbsp. of Garlic
- 1 tsp. of Cumin
- 1 tsp. of paprika
- ½ tsp. of Cayenne pepper
- 2 tbsp. of ground fennel
- 1 tbsp. of finely chopped cilantro
- 1 tbsp. of finely chopped parsley
- 1 tsp. of black pepper
- 1 Pinch of black pepper
- 2 tbsp. of salt
- For the Sauce:
- 3 Cups of Greek Yogurt
- 1 Juiced Lemon
- 1 Garlic clove
- 1 Peeled, drained and shredded cucumber
- 1 tbsp. of dill
- 1 Pinch of salt
- 1 Pinch of pepper

Braised Lamb 'n Apricot

NUTRITION

Calories: 250, Fat: 18g,
Carbohydrates: 6g, Protein: 21g

INTOLERANCES

Gluten-Free
Egg-Free
Lactose-Free

DIRECTIONS

15 MINUTES

3 HOUR

7

SHOPPING LIST

- 1 Leg of lamb of about 4 to 6 lbs. with the aitchbone removed
- Green Mountain Wild Game Rub
- 2 tbsp. of minced garlic
- For the Apricot-Mustard Glaze:
- 1 Jar of about 10 Oz of apricot jelly
- 1/4 Cup of yellow mustard
- 1 tsp. of garlic powder

1. Start by rubbing the lamb generously with the Wild Game Rub and the minced garlic.
2. Grill at a temperature of about 400°F for about 30 minutes, turning at least once
3. While the lamb is being cooked, combine the ingredients of the Glaze in a medium saucepan and let simmer for about 15 minutes.
4. Decrease the heat to about 325°F and cook for about 60 minutes or until the internal temperature of the meat reaches about 130°F
5. Reduce the heat on the grill to 325 and cook for about 60 minutes
6. Brush the lamb with the prepared glaze for a few times during the last 30 minutes.
7. Remove the lamb meat from the wood pellet grill and cover with a foil for about 10 minutes.
8. Serve and enjoy your dish!

Spiced Lamb Kabobs

 NUTRITION

Calories: 170, Fat: 9g,
Carbohydrates: 3g, Protein: 20g

 INTOLERANCES

Gluten-Free   Lactose-Free
Egg-Free

 6
 30 MINUTES
 40 MINUTES

SHOPPING LIST

- 1 ¼ Cup of olive oil
- 1 ¼ Cup of sherry
- 2 Medium jumbo red onions
- 1 tbsp. of GMG Wild Game Rub
- 1 tbsp. of freshly ground black pepper
- 5 Garlic cloves
- 1 Leg of Lamb of about 3 to 4 pounds

DIRECTIONS

1. Start by trimming the fat cap from the lamb meat and cut the meat into cubes of about 1 ½ inches each.
2. Place the meat into a bowl and sprinkle the rub on top of the meat; toss very well until your ingredients are mixed and if you don't have this type of Rub you can substitute it with 1 teaspoon of sugar, 1 teaspoon of salt, ¼ teaspoon of fresh ginger, and about ¼ teaspoon of the turmeric.
3. You can chop some sprigs of fresh parsley; then add it to the onion.
4. In another separate bowl; combine 1 cup of olive oil with 1 cup of sherry and about 1 tablespoon of ground black pepper.
5. Peel about 5 garlic cloves and press it to ash very well.
6. Add in the garlic and beat very well until it becomes frothy; then mix.
7. Add the onion mixture on top of the lamb and cubes; then cover and refrigerate for an overnight.
8. Skewer the chunks of lamb on 2 skewers.
9. Pack the meat tightly; then grill at a temperature of about 360 to 380°F for about 25 to 35 minutes
10. Let the meat rest for about 5 minutes.
11. Serve and enjoy your dish!

Lamb Ribs with Herbs

NUTRITION

Calories: 265, Fat: 10g, 13g, Carbohydrates: Protein: 26g

15 MINUTES

INTOLERANCES

Gluten-Free
Egg-Free
Lactose-Free

4 HOUR

SHOPPING LIST

- 4 Racks of Raider Red Lamb Riblets
- For the marinade:
- 1/2 Cup of olive oil
- 4 Juiced large lemons
- 1 and ½ cups of smoked garlic cloves
- 3 tbsp. of dry Chinese mustard
- 2 tbsp. of dried Tarragon
- 2 tbsp. of Date Night Heat seasoning

DIRECTIONS

1. Combine the marinade in your food processor and mix all the ingredients until your get a liquefied mixture.
2. Score the lamb ribs in a shape of a diamond cut in order to allow the fats to render some of it and let the marinade penetrate the lamb ribs.
3. Place the ribs in a large plastic container or in an extra-large freezer bag; then pour the marinade on top. Refrigerate for about 48 hours.
4. Once ready to cook your meat, preheat your wood pellet smoker grill to a temperature of about 250°F.
5. When the smoker grill is hot; place the ribs with the bone side down for about 3 hours.
6. Spoon the prepared marinade right on top of the ribs in order to create a nice and crusty topping.
7. When the ribs of lamb reach an internal temperature of about 190°F; pull off the lamb ribs and cover; then let rest for about 5 to 10 minutes.
8. Feel free to combine your favorite types of wood pellets and make sure to smoke the meat at a temperature that is less than 250°F.
9. Let the meat rest for about 5 to 10 minutes.
10. Serve and enjoy your dish!

Greek Style Roast Leg of Lamb

 NUTRITION

Calories: 760, Fat: 64g,
Cholesterol: 190mg,
Carbs: 1g, Protein: 40g

 INTOLERANCES

Gluten-Free
Egg-Free
Lactose-Free

 **SHOPPING LIST**

- 6 tablespoons extra-virgin olive oil
- 1 Leg of lamb (6 to 7 pounds), bone-in
- Juice of 2 lemons, freshly squeezed
- 2 sprigs of fresh rosemary, stems discarded, stripped needles
- 1 sprig of fresh oregano, or 1 teaspoon Dried
- 8 garlic cloves
- Freshly ground black pepper and kosher salt (coarse) as required

 DIRECTIONS

1. Make a chain of small slits in the meat using a sharp paring knife.
For herb and garlic paste:
2. Finely mince the rosemary with oregano, and garlic using a chef's knife on a clean, large cutting board. Alternatively, add these ingredients in a food processor.
3. Stuff some of the prepared paste into each of the slits on meat; ensure that you add it into the slit using any of the utensils.
4. Add the coated lamb on a rack, preferably inside a large roasting pan. For easier clean-up; don't forget to line the pan with aluminum foil.

5. Rub the outside of meat first with the freshly squeezed lemon juice and then with the olive oil. Using a plastic wrap; cover and refrigerate for overnight.
6. The following day; remove the meat from refrigerator and let sit at room temperature for half an hour.
7. Get rid of the plastic wrap and season the meat with pepper and salt to taste.
8. When ready, preheat the grill of wood pellet on Smoke for 4 to 5 minutes, with the lid open. Set the cooking temperature to 400°F and close the lid.
9. Roast the lamb for half an hour.

Decrease the heat to 350°F and continue cooking for an hour more, until the internal temperature of the meat reflects 140°F.

10. Transfer the cooked lamb to a large, clean cutting board and let rest for a couple of minutes then, slice diagonally into thin slices.

11. Serve while still hot and enjoy.

25 MINUTES

1.h 35 MINUTES

Classic Rosemary Lamb

 **NUTRITION**

Calories: 660, Fat: 57g,
Cholesterol: 150mg, Carbs: 17g,
Protein: 20g

 INTOLERANCES:

Gluten-Free
Egg-Free

20 MINUTES

3 HR 15 MINUTES

SHOPPING LIST

- 1 rack lamb, rib
- A bunch of fresh asparagus
- 2 rosemary,
- springs
- 1 dozen baby potato
- 2 tablespoons
- olive oil
- Pepper and salt to taste
- 1/2 cup butter

2

 DIRECTIONS

1. Preheat the grill of your wood pellet to 225°F in advance.
2. Get rid of the membrane from the back side of the ribs and then, drizzle on both sides with olive oil; finally sprinkle with the rosemary.
3. Combine the butter with potatoes in a deep baking dish.
4. Place the rack of prepared ribs alongside the dish of potatoes on the grates. Smoke until the internal temperature of the meat reflects 145°F, for 3 hours.
5. During the last 15 minutes of cooking don't forget to add asparagus to the potatoes and continue to cook until turn tender.
6. Slice the lamb into desired pieces and serve with cooked asparagus and potatoes.

Smoked Rack of Lamb

 **NUTRITION**

Calories: 780, Fat: 60g,
Cholesterol: 200mg, Carbs: 5g,
Protein: 50g

 INTOLERANCES:

Gluten-Free
Egg-Free
Lactose-Free

20 MINUTES

 4

 1 HR 20 MINUTES

 SHOPPING LIST

- A rack of lamb, preferably 4 to 5 pounds
- For Marinade
- 1 medium lemon
- 4 garlic cloves, minced
- 1 teaspoon thyme
- 1/4 cup balsamic vinegar
- 1 teaspoon basil
- 1 teaspoon each of pepper and salt
- For Glaze
- 2 tablespoons soy sauce
- 1/4 cup Dijon mustard
- 2 tablespoons Worcestershire sauce
- 1/4 cup dry red wine

DIRECTIONS

1. Combine the entire marinade ingredients together in a gallon-sized zip lock bag.
2. Once done, trim the silver skin from the lamb racks and then, add the trimmed racks into the gallon bag with the marinade; mix the pieces well and refrigerate for overnight.
3. The following day preheat your wood pellet to 300°F in advance. In the meantime, combine the entire glaze ingredients together in a large-sized mixing bowl.
4. Once the glaze is mixed and the grill is preheated, place the rack of lamb over the hot grill.
5. Cook the racks for 12 to 15 minutes and then, baste with the prepared glaze mixture.
6. Flip and cook the meat until the internal temperature reflects somewhere between 135 to 145°F, approximately for an hour; don't forget to baste the meat with the glaze after every half an hour.
7. Once done, remove the meat from grill and let sit for a couple of minutes.
8. Cut the meat into desired pieces; serve hot and enjoy.

Smoked Loin Lamb

📖 NUTRITION

Calories: 650, Fat: 50g,
Cholesterol: 155mg, Carbs: 1g,
Protein: 42g

📖 INTOLERANCES:

Gluten-Free
Egg-Free
Lactose-Free

20 MINUTES

1 HR 20 MINUTES

6

🧺 SHOPPING LIST

- 10 to 12 Lamb loin chops
- Jeff's Original rub recipe
- Rosemary , finely chopped
- Olive oil
- Coarse kosher salt

🛍️ DIRECTIONS

1. Place the chops on a cookie sheet or cooling rack.
2. To dry brine, generously sprinkle the top of chops with salt.
3. Place in a fridge for an hour or two.
4. Once done; remove the coated meat from fridge; ensure that you don't rinse the meat.
5. Prepare an infusion of olive oil and rosemary by pouring approximately ¼ cup of the olive oil on top of 1 tablespoon of the chopped rosemary; set the mixture aside and let sit for an hour.
6. Brush the prepared mixture on top and sides of your lamb chops.
7. Generously sprinkle the top, sides and bottom of chops with the rub.
8. Preheat your smoker at 225°F on indirect heat.
9. For great results, ensure that you use a mixture of apple and pecan for smoke.
10. Cook the coated chops for 40 to 50 minutes, until the internal temperature of chops reflects 138°F.
11. Let rest on the counter for 5 to 7 minutes, with foil tented.
12. Serve hot and enjoy.

CHAPTER 6

Poultry Recipes

Teriyaki Chicken Wings 'n Sesame Dressing

SHOPPING LIST

- Chicken wings
- 2/3 cup mirin
- 2 tbsp of minced ginger
- 3 tbsp of cornstarch
- 2 tbsp of rice vinegar
- 1 cup of soy sauce
- 1/3 cup of brown sugar
- 8 minced garlic cloves

- 2 tsp of sesame oil
- 3 tbsp of water

For Creamy Sesame Dressing:
- 1 green onion, chopped
- 1/2 cup of mayonnaise
- 1/4 cup rice wine vinegar

- 1 tsp of ground garlic
- 1 tbsp of soy sauce
- 2 tbsp of sesame oil
- 1/2 tsp of ground ginger
- 1 tsp siracha
- 2 tbsp of maple syrup
- Salt and pepper to taste

1 HR 10 MINUTES

20 MINUTES

6

DIRECTIONS

1. Use light pellets for the sake of getting the smoky flavor.
2. Set the grill to smoke mode by keeping the temperature to 225°F.
3. Now trim the wings and make them into drumettes and season with sea salt and black pepper.
4. Smoke them for about 45 minutes. For the teriyaki glaze:
5. Mince both garlic and ginger and add a teaspoon of sesame oil.
6. Then mix all the ingredients except for cornstarch and water.
7. Take a pan and boil the cornstarch and water on low heat.
8. Simmer for 15 minutes and then, when done, pass it through a blender.
9. Add this mix to the teriyaki glaze and mix it well until it thickens. Set it aside.
10. For the creamy dressing: Take a blender and blend all the ingredients thoroughly until you get a smooth mixture.
11. Set the grill to direct flame grilling and put the temperature to medium.
12. Grill the wings for approximately 10 minutes.
13. The internal temperature should reach 165°F when you remove the wings from the grill.
14. Toss them in the glaze when done.
15. Sprinkle some sesame seeds along with the green onion.
16. Serve hot and spicy.

Smoked Turkey Legs

20 MINUTES

4

4-5 HOUR

🧺 SHOPPING LIST

- 4 turkey legs
- 2 bay leaves
- 1 cup of BBQ rubs
- 1 tbsp of crushed allspice berries
- 2 tsp of liquid smoke
- ½ gal of cold water
- 4 cups of ice
- 1 gal of warm water
- ½ cup of brown
- sugar
- ½ cup of curing salt
- 1 tbsp of peppercorns; whole black

🛍 DIRECTIONS

1. Take a large stockpot and mix a gallon of warm water to curing salt, rub, peppercorns, brown sugar, liquid smoke, allspice and bay leaves
2. Bring this mix to boil by keeping the flame on high heat and let all salt granules dissolve thoroughly. Let it cool to room temperature.
3. Add ice and cold water and let the whole thing chill in the refrigerator.
4. Add turkey legs and make sure they are submerged in the brine. Let it stay for a day.
5. Now drain the turkey legs and get rid of the brine.
6. Wash off the brine from the legs with the help of cold water and then pat it dry.
7. Set the grill to preheat by keeping the temperature to 250°F.
8. Lay the legs directly on the grate of the grill.
9. Smoke it for 4 to 5 hours till the internal temperature reaches 165°F.
10. Serve and enjoy.

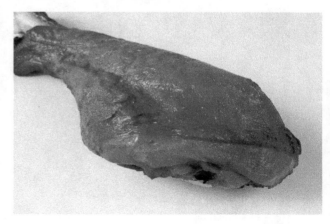

Lemony Chicken

Calories: 178, Fat: 9g,
Protein: 23g

INTOLERANCES:

Gluten-Free
Egg-Free
Lactose-Free

20 MINUTES

4

SHOPPING LIST

- 1 whole chicken
- 4 cloves of minced garlic
- Zest of 2 fresh lemons
- 1 tbsp of olive oil
- 1 tbsp of smoked paprika
- 1 ½ tsp of salt
- ½ tsp of black pepper
- ½ tsp of dried oregano
- 1 tbsp of ground cumin

DIRECTIONS

1. Preheat the grill to a temperature of 375°F.
2. Take the chicken and cut it on both sides right from the backbone to the tail via the neck.
3. Lay it flat and push it down on the breastbone. This would break the ribs.
4. Take all the leftover ingredients in a bowl except ½ tsp of salt and crush them to make a smooth rub.
5. Spread this rub evenly over the chicken, making sure that it seeps right under the skin.
6. Place the chicken on the grill grates and cook for an hour until the internal temperature reads 165°F. Let it rest for 10 minutes.
7. Serve and enjoy.

1 HR 10 MINUTES

Slow Roasted Shawarma

📖 NUTRITION

Calories: 585, Fat: 40g,
Carbs: 9g, Protein: 46g

📖 INTOLERANCES:

Egg-Free
Lactose-Free

20 MINUTES

4 HR 10 MINUTES

🧺 SHOPPING LIST

- 5 ½ lbs. of chicken thighs; boneless, skinless
- 4 ½ lbs. of lamb fat
- Pita bread
- 5 ½ lbs. of top sirloin
- 2 yellow onions; large
- 4 tbsp of rub
- Desired toppings like pickles, tomatoes, fries, salad and more

🛍 DIRECTIONS

1. Slice the meat and fat into ½" slices and place then in 3 separate bowls.
2. Season each of the bowls with the rub and massage them into the meat to make sure it seeps well.
3. Place half of the onion at the base of each half skewer.
4. Add 2 layers from each of the bowls at a time.
5. Put the other 2 half onions at the top, wrap it in plastic and let it refrigerate overnight.
6. Set the grill to preheat, keeping the temperature to 275°F.
7. Lay the shawarma on the grill grate and let it cook for approximately 4 hours. Make sure to turn it at least once.
8. Remove from the grill and shoot the temperature to 445°F. Place a cast iron griddle on the grill grate and pour it with olive oil.
9. When the griddle has turned hot, place the whole shawarma on the cast iron and smoke it for 5 to 10 minutes per side.
10. Remove from the grill and slice off the edges. Repeat the same with the leftover shawarma.
11. Serve in pita bread and add the chosen toppings.

Duck Poppers

NUTRITION

Calories: 337 Fat: 30g,
Cholesterol: 143mg, Carbs: 19g,
Protein: 12g

INTOLERANCES:

Gluten-Free
Egg-Free
Lactose-Free

15 MINUTES

30 MINUTES

SHOPPING LIST

- 8 – 10 pieces of bacon, cut event into same-sized pieces measuring 4 inches each
- 3 duck breasts; boneless and with skin removed and sliced into strips measuring ½ inches
- Sriracha sauce
- 6 de-seeded jalapenos, with the top cut off and sliced into strips

DIRECTIONS

1. Wrap the bacon around one trip of pepper and one slice of duck.
2. Secure it firmly with the help of a toothpick.
3. Fire the grill on low flame and keep this wrap and grill it for half an hour until the bacon turns crisp.
4. Rotate often to ensure even cooking.
5. Serve with sriracha sauce.

BBQ Pulled Turkey Sandwiches

 NUTRITION

Calories: 289, Fat: 10g,
Cholesterol: 80mg,
Carbs: 23g, Protein: 26g

INTOLERANCES:

Gluten-Free
Egg-Free

15 MINUTES

1 HOUR

6

SHOPPING LIST

- 6 skin-on turkey thighs
- 6 split and buttered buns
- 1 ½ cups of chicken broth
- 1 cup of BBQ sauce
- Poultry rub

DIRECTIONS

1. Season the turkey thighs on both sides with poultry rub.
2. Set the grill to preheat by pushing the temperature to 180°F.
3. Arrange the turkey thighs on the grate of the grill and smoke it for 30 minutes.
4. Transfer the thighs to an aluminum foil which is disposable and then pour the brine right around the thighs. Cover it with a lid.
5. Increase the grill temperature to 325°F and roast the thigh till the internal temperature reaches 180°F.
6. Remove the foil from the grill, but do not turn off the grill. Let the turkey thighs cool down a little.
7. Pour the dripping and serve. Remove the skin and discard it.
8. Pull the meat into shreds and return it to the foil.
9. Add 1 more cup of BBQ sauce and some more dripping.
10. Cover the foil with lid and re-heat the turkey on the smoker for half an hour.
11. Serve and enjoy.

Baked Garlic Parmesan Wings

 NUTRITION

Calories: 90, Fat: 8g, Cholesterol: 22mg, Carbs: 1g, Protein: 4g

 INTOLERANCES

Gluten-Free
Egg-Free

20 MINUTES

30 MINUTES

 **SHOPPING LIST**

- 5 lbs. of chicken wings
- ½ cup of chicken rub

For the garnish:
- 1 cup of shredded parmesan cheese
- 3 tbsp of chopped parsley

For the Sauce:
- 10 cloves of finely diced garlic
- 1 cup of butter
- 2 tbsp of chicken rub

 DIRECTIONS

1. Set the grill on preheat by keeping the temperature high.
2. Take a large bowl and toss the wings in it along with the chicken rub.
3. Place the wings directly on the grill grate and cook it for 10 minutes.
4. Flip it and cook for the next ten minutes.
5. Check the internal temperature, and it needs to reach in the range of 165 to 180°F.

For the garlic Sauce:

6. Take a midsized saucepan and mix garlic, butter, and the leftover rub.
7. Cook it over medium heat on a stovetop for 10 minutes while stirring in between to avoid the making of lumps.
8. When the wings have been cooked, remove them from the grill and place in a large bowl.
9. Toss the wings with garlic sauce along with parsley and parmesan cheese.
10. Serve and enjoy.

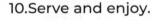
4

Cajun Chicken

4

30 MINUTES

DIRECTIONS

1. Place the chicken breast on a cutting board with the chest down.
2. Using kitchen or poultry scissors, cut along the side of the spine and remove.
3. Turn the chicken over and press down firmly on the chest to flatten it. Carefully loosen and remove the skin on the chest, thighs and drumsticks.
4. Rub olive oil freely under and on the skin. Season chicken in all directions and apply directly to the meat under the skin.
5. Wrap the chicken in plastic wrap and place in the refrigerator for 3 hours to absorb the flavor.
6. Use hickory, pecan pellets, or blend to configure a wood pellet smoker grill for indirect cooking and preheat to 225°F.
7. If the unit has a temperature meat probe input, such as a MAK Grills 2 Star, insert the probe into the thickest part of the breast. Make chicken for 1 1/2 hours.
8. After one and a half hours at 225°F, raise the pit temperature to 375°F and roast until the inside temperature of the thickest part of the chest reaches 170°F and the thighs are at least 180°F.
9. Place the chicken under a loose foil tent for 15 minutes before carving.

2 HR 30 MINUTES

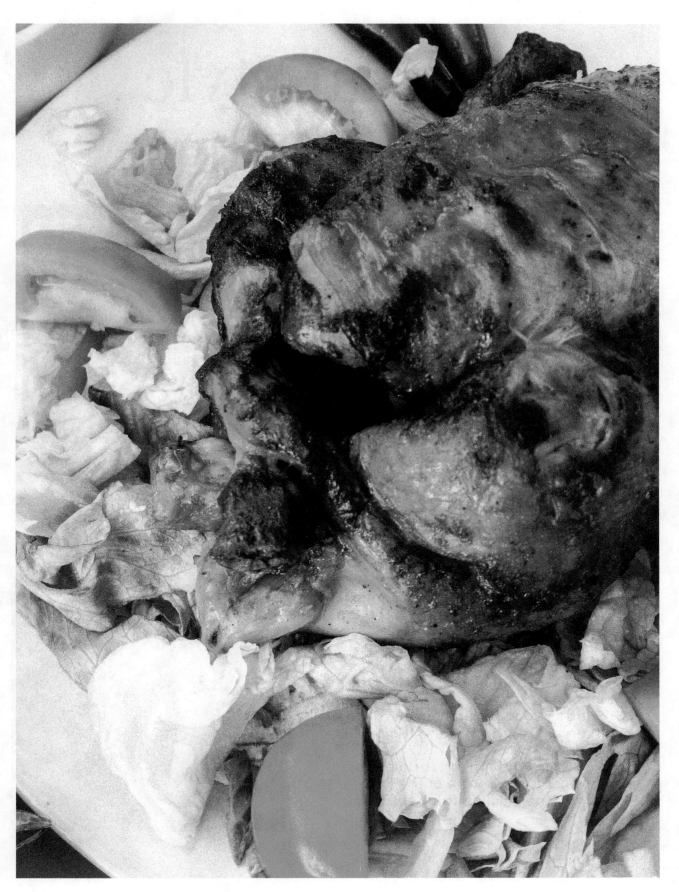

Tuscan Style Roasted Thighs

 NUTRITION

Calories: 308, Fat: 18g,
Carbs: 1g, Protein: 30g

 INTOLERANCES

Gluten-Free
Egg-Free
Lactose-Free

 DIRECTIONS

4

10 MINUTES

1 HOUR

 **SHOPPING LIST**

- 8 chicken thighs, with bone, with skin
- 3 extra virgin olive oils with roasted garlic flavor
- 3 cups of Tuscan or Tuscan seasoning per thigh

1. Cut off excess skin on chicken thighs and leave at 1/4 inch to shrink.
2. Carefully peel off the skin and remove large deposits of fat under the skin and behind the thighs.
3. Lightly rub olive oil behind and below the skin and thighs. A seasoning from Tuscan, seasoned on the skin of the thigh and the top and bottom of the back.
4. Wrap chicken thighs in plastic wrap, refrigerate for 1-2 hours, allow time for flavor to be absorbed before roasting.
5. Set the wood pellet smoker grill for indirect cooking and use the pellets to preheat to 375°F.
6. Roast for 40-60 minutes until the internal temperature of the thick part of the chicken thigh reaches 180°F.
7. Place the roasted Tuscan thighs under a loose foil tent for 15 minutes before serving.

Teriyaki Smoking Drumsticks

 NUTRITION

Calories: 340, Fat: 9g,
Cholesterol: 114mgCarbs: 16g,
Protein: 45g

 INTOLERANCES

Gluten-Free
Egg-Free
Lactose-Free

 15 MINUTES

 1 HR 40 MINUTES

 4

SHOPPING LIST

- 3 cup of teriyaki marinade and cooking sauce like Yoshida's original gourmet
- Poultry seasoning 3 tsp
- 1 tsp garlic powder
- 10 chicken drumsticks

 DIRECTIONS

1. In a medium bowl, mix the marinade and cooking sauce with the chicken seasoning and garlic powder.
2. Peel off the skin of the drumsticks to promote marinade penetration.
3. Put the drumsticks in a marinade pan or large plastic sealable bag and pour the marinade mixture. Refrigerate overnight.
4. Rotate the chicken leg in the morning.
5. Set the wood pellet smoking grill for indirect cooking.
6. Pat dry the drumsticks with a kitchen paper towel to remove excess liquid. Then place the skins back on the drumsticks.
7. Preheat the wood pellet smoker grill to 180°F using hickory or maple pellets.
8. Cook the marinated chicken legs for 1 hour.
9. After 1 hour, raise the whole temperature to 350°F and cook the drumsticks for another 30-45 minutes until the thickest part reaches an internal temperature of 180°F.
10. Remove from the grill and allow the drumsticks to cool slightly before serving.

Smoked Bone–in–Turkey Breast

NUTRITION

Calories: 70, Fat: 2g,
Carbs: 1g, Protein: 12g

INTOLERANCES

Gluten-Free
Egg-Free
Lactose-Free

6-8

SHOPPING LIST

- 1 (8-10 pounds) boned turkey breast
- 6 tablespoons extra virgin olive oil
- 5 Yang original dry lab or poultry seasonings

DIRECTIONS

1. Remove excess fat and skin from turkey breast.
2. Carefully separate the skin from the breast and leave the skin alone. Apply olive oil to the chest, under the skin and on the skin.
3. Rub or season carefully under the chest cavity, under the skin and on the skin.
4. Place the turkey breast in a V-rack for easy handling or place it directly on a grill grate with the breast up.
5. Rest the turkey breasts on the kitchen counter at room temperature and preheat the wood pellet smoker grill.
6. Configure a wood pellet smoker grill for indirect cooking and preheat to 225°F using hickory or pecan pellets.
7. Smoke the boned turkey breast directly in a V rack or grill at 225°F for 2 hours.
8. After 2 hours of hickory smoke, raise the pit temperature to 325°F. Roast until the thickest part of the turkey breast reaches an internal temperature of 170°F and the juice is clear.
9. Place the hickory smoked turkey breast under a loose foil tent for 20 minutes, then scrape the grain.

20
MINUTES

3- 4
HOUR

Bacon Cordon Bleu

 NUTRITION

Calories: 230, Fat: 2g, Cholesterol: 78mg, Carbs: 13g, Protein: 38g

 INTOLERANCES

Gluten-Free
Egg-Free

6

 DIRECTIONS

1. Weave 4 slices of bacon tightly, leaving extra space on the edges. Bacon weave is used to interlock alternating bacon slices and wrap chicken cordon blue.
2. Slice or rub two chicken breast fillets with olive oil on both sides.
3. Sprinkle the seasoning on both sides of the chicken breast.
4. Lay the seasoned chicken fillets on the bacon weave and slice one ham and one provolone cheese on each.
5. Repeat this process with another chicken fillet, ham and cheese. Fold chicken, ham and cheese in half.
6. Lay the bacon strips from the opposite corner to completely cover the chicken cordon blue.
7. Use a silicon food grade cooking band, butcher twine, and toothpick to secure the bacon strip in place.
8. Repeat this process for the remaining chicken breast and ingredients.

SHOPPING LIST

- 24 bacon slices
- 3 large boneless, skinless chicken breasts, butterfly
- 3 extra virgin olive oils with roasted garlic flavor
- 3 Yang original dry lab or poultry seasonings
- 12 slice black forest ham
- 12-slice provolone cheese

9. Using apple or cherry pellets, configure a wood pellet smoker grill for indirect cooking and preheat (180°F to 200°F) for smoking. Inhale bacon cordon blue for 1 hour.
10. After smoking for 1 hour, raise the pit temperature to 350°F.
11. Bacon cordon blue occurs when the internal temperature reaches 165°F and the bacon becomes crispy.
12. Rest for 15 minutes under a loose foil tent before serving.

30 MINUTES

2 HOUR

Lemon Cornish Chicken Stuffed with Crab Meat

30 MINUTES

 NUTRITION

Calories: 660, Fat: 47g,
Protein: 57g

 INTOLERANCES

Gluten-Free
Egg-Free

DIRECTIONS

2-4

2 HOUR

SHOPPING LIST

- 24 bacon slices
- 3 large boneless, skinless chicken breasts, butterfly
- 3 extra virgin olive oils with roasted garlic flavor
- 3 Yang original dry lab or poultry seasonings
- 12 slice black forest ham
- 12-slice provolone cheese

1. Weave 4 slices of bacon tightly, leaving extra space on the edges. Bacon weave is used to interlock alternating bacon slices and wrap chicken cordon blue.
2. Slice or rub two chicken breast fillets with olive oil on both sides.
3. Sprinkle the seasoning on both sides of the chicken breast.
4. Lay the seasoned chicken fillets on the bacon weave and slice one ham and one provolone cheese on each.
5. Repeat this process with another chicken fillet, ham and cheese. Fold chicken, ham and cheese in half.
6. Lay the bacon strips from the opposite corner to completely cover the chicken cordon blue.
7. Use a silicon food grade cooking band, butcher twine, and toothpick to secure the bacon strip in place.
8. Repeat this process for the remaining chicken breast and ingredients.
9. Using apple or cherry pellets,

configure a wood pellet smoker grill for indirect cooking and preheat (180°F to 200°F) for smoking. Inhale bacon cordon blue for 1 hour.
10. After smoking for 1 hour, raise the pit temperature to 350°F.
11. Bacon cordon blue occurs when the internal temperature reaches 165°F and the bacon becomes crispy.
12. Rest for 15 minutes under a loose foil tent before serving.

Roast Duck a L'Orange

 NUTRITION

Calories: 467, Fat: 24g,
Cholesterol: 221mg,
Carbs: 6g, Protein: 51g

 INTOLERANCES

Gluten-Free
Egg-Free

 DIRECTIONS

1. Remove the nibble from the duck's cavity and neck. Rinse the duck and pat dry with a paper towel.
2. Remove excess fat from tail, neck and cavity. Use a sharp scalpel knife tip to pierce the duck's skin entirely, so that it does not penetrate the duck's meat, to help dissolve the fat layer beneath the skin.
3. Add the seasoning inside the cavity with one cup of rub or seasoning.
4. Season the outside of the duck with the remaining friction or seasoning.
5. Fill the cavity with orange wedges, celery and onion. Duck legs are tied with butcher twine to make filling easier. Place the duck breast up on a small rack of shallow roast bread.
6. To make the sauce, mix the ingredients in the saucepan over low heat and cook until the sauce is thick and syrupy. Set aside and let cool.
7. Set the wood pellet smoker grill for indirect cooking and use the pellets to preheat to 350°F.
8. Roast the ducks at 350°F for 2 hours.
9. After 2 hours, brush the duck freely with orange sauce.
10. Roast the orange glass duck for another 30 minutes, making sure that the inside temperature of the thickest part of the leg reaches 165°F.
11. Place duck under loose foil tent for 20 minutes before serving.
12. Serve.

4

30 MINUTES

2.5 HOUR

SHOPPING LIST

- 1 (5-6 lb.) Frozen Long Island, Beijing or Canadian ducks
- 3 tbsp west or 3 tbsp
- 1 large orange, cut into wedges
- 3 celery stems chopped into large chunks
- 1/2 small red onion, a quarter

- Orange Sauce:
- 2 orange cups
- 2 tablespoons soy sauce
- 2 tablespoons orange marmalade
- 2 tablespoons honey
- 3g tsp grated raw

Flattened Mojo Chicken

NUTRITION

Calories: 160, Fat: 10g,
Carbs: 1g, Protein: 20g

INTOLERANCES

Gluten-Free
Egg-Free

25 MINUTES

1 HOUR

6

SHOPPING LIST

- 3 – 4 lb. whole chickens
- 3 tbsp. olive oil
- 6 cups Traditional Cuban Mojo
- 3 tsp. sea salt
- 3 tbsp. Adobo Criollo spices

DIRECTIONS

1. Rinse chicken with cold water and pat dry. Cut out backbone with kitchen shears.
2. Turn chicken breast side up and open like a book. Press down firmly on breast to flatten and break rib bones. Loosen skin from body under breast and thighs.
3. Place each chicken in a gallon-size resealable bag with 2 cups Mojo. Marinate (flat) in refrigerator 24 hours. Remove chickens from bags and discard mojo.
4. Blot each bird dry, and rub each with 1 Tbsp. olive oil, and then 1 Tbsp. Adobo Criollo spice blend.
5. Pre-heat one side of your pellet grill; and leave one side unlighted, cover and preheat for 20 minutes.
6. Place chicken skin side down in the middle of the grill with legs closest to the heat.
7. Watch carefully and turn over when skin starts to brown. Turn and move chicken to the "cool" side and cover with a large disposable aluminum pan (a favorite restaurant trick.)

8. Cooking time will vary, depending on the fire and the size of the chicken.
9. Check the temperature at 20 minutes after turning. When the temperature in the thigh reaches 175 degrees, remove from the heat and let sit, loosely covered for 15 minutes.

Sizzling' Buffalo Wings

 NUTRITION

Calories: 130, Fat: 6g,
Carbs: 6g, Protein: 10g

 INTOLERANCES

Gluten-Free
Egg-Free

 8

 10 MINUTES

 40 MINUTES

 DIRECTIONS

1. Mix all except chicken, salt, oil and flour in a pan, bring to a simmer, stirring, and then cool.
2. Toss the wings with the oil, and salt. Place into a large plastic bag, add the flour, and shake to coat evenly. Remove from the bag, shaking off excess flour.
3. Place wings on hot pellet grill, turning several times until golden brown.
4. Remove wings from grill and place them in a sealed bowl with the sauce and shake well.
5. Serve immediately with blue cheese and chilled celery sticks.

SHOPPING LIST

- 36 chicken wings, separated
- 1 tbsp. vegetable oil
- 1 tsp. salt
- 1 cup all-purpose flour
- 1 ½ tbsp. white vinegar
- 1/4 tsp. cayenne pepper
- 1/4 tsp. garlic powder
- 1 tsp. Tabasco sauce
- 1/4 tsp. Worcestershire sauce
- 1/4 tsp. seasoned salt
- 6 tbsp. Frank's Red-Hot Sauce
- 6 tbsp. unsalted butter
- Celery sticks and blue cheese dressing

Chicken with Peanut Sauce

📖 NUTRITION

Calories: 185, Fat: 9g,
Carbs: 5g, Protein: 20g

📖 INTOLERANCES:

Gluten-Free
Egg-Free

8   20 MINUTES   40 MINUTES

🧺 SHOPPING LIST

- 4 tbsp. olive oil
- 4 tbsp. sesame oil
- 2 tsp. ginger powder
- 2 tsp. powdered garlic
- 2 tbsp. curry powder
  Butter lettuce leaves
- 20 wooden skewers,

  soaked Fresh cilantro leaves
- 2 lbs. chicken thighs, cut into strips

Peanut Sauce:
- 2 cups chunky peanut butter

- 1/2 cups soy sauce
- 1/4 cup brown sugar
- 1/4 cup sweet chili paste
- 1/3 cup limes juice
- 2/3 cup hot water

🛍 DIRECTIONS

1. Combine oils, ginger, garlic, and curry powder in a shallow mixing bowl. Place the chicken strips in the marinade and gently toss until well coated.
2. Cover and let the chicken marinate in the refrigerator overnight.
3. Thread the chicken pieces onto the soaked skewers working the skewer in and out of the meat, down the middle of the piece, so that it stays in place during grilling.
4. Brush pellet grill with oil to prevent the meat from sticking. Grill the satays for 3 to 5 minutes on each side, until nicely seared and cooked through.
5. Serve on a platter lined with lettuce leaves and cilantro; accompanied by a small bowl of peanut sauce on the side.

For the Sauce:

6. Combine the peanut butter, soy sauce, chili paste, brown sugar, and lime juice in a food processor or blender. Puree to combine, and drizzle in the hot water to thin out the sauce.
7. Pour the sauce into individual serving bowls.
8. Enjoy!!

CHAPTER 7

Pork Recipes

Pork Burnt Ends

NUTRITION

Calories: 477, Fat: 41.8g,
Cholesterol: 58mg,
Carbohydrate: 19.3g, Protein: 6.4g

INTOLERANCES:

Gluten-Free
Egg-Free

 15 MINUTES
 4.30 MINUTES
 10

SHOPPING LIST

- 4 pounds pork belly
- 4 tbsp brown sugar
- ¼ tsp cayenne pepper
- 1 tsp red pepper flakes
- ½ tsp onion powder
- ½ tsp garlic powder
- 1 tbsp paprika
- 1 tsp oregano
- 1 tbsp freshly ground black pepper
- 2 tbsp salt or to taste
- 1 tsp dried peppermint
- 2 tbsp olive oil
- ¼ cup butter
- 1 cup BBQ sauce
- 4 tbsp maple syrup
- 2 tbsp chopped fresh parsley

DIRECTIONS

1. Trim pork belly of any excess fat and cut off silver skin. Cut the pork into ½ inch cubes.
2. To make rub, combine the sugar, cayenne, pepper flakes, onion powder, garlic, paprika, oregano, black pepper, salt, and peppermint in a mixing bowl.
3. Drizzle oil over the pork and season each pork cubes generously with the rub.
4. Preheat your grill to 205°F with lid closed for 15 minutes.
5. Arrange the pork chunks onto the grill grate and smoke for about 3 hours, or until the pork chunks turn dark red.
6. Meanwhile, combine the BBQ sauce, maple syrup and butter in an aluminum pan.
7. Remove the pork slices from heat and put them in the pan with the sauce. Stir to combine.
8. Cover the pan tightly with aluminum foil and place it on the grill. Cook for 1 hour or until the internal temperature of the pork reaches 200°F.
9. Remove the pork from heat and let it sit for some minutes.
10. Serve and garnish with fresh chopped parsley.

British Pork Belly

 **NUTRITION**

Calories: 430 Cal

Fat: 44 g

Carbs: 1 g

Protein: 8 g

Fiber: 0 g

INTOLERANCES:

Gluten-Free

Egg-Free

6   10 MINUTES

3H 30M

SHOPPING LIST

- 3 pounds pork belly, skin removed
- Pork and poultry rub as needed
- 4 tablespoons salt
- 1/2 teaspoon ground black pepper

DIRECTIONS

1. Switch on the Smoker grill, fill the grill hopper with apple-flavored wood pellets, power the grill on by using the control panel, select 'smoke' on the temperature dial, or set the temperature to 275 degrees F and let it preheat for a minimum of 15 minutes.
2. Meanwhile, prepare the pork belly and for this, sprinkle pork and poultry rub, salt, and black pepper on all sides of pork belly until well coated.
3. When the grill has preheated, open the lid, place the pork belly on the grill grate, shut the grill and smoke for 3 hours and 30 minutes until the internal temperature reaches 200 degrees F.
4. When done, transfer the pork belly to a cutting board, let it rest for 15 minutes, then cut it into slices and serve.

Cherry & Jalapeño Ribs

15 MINUTES

 **NUTRITION**

Calories: 267, Fat: 18g,
Carbs: 3g, Protein: 16g

 **INTOLERANCES:**

Gluten-Free
Egg-Free
Lactose-Free

6 HOURS

4

🧺 **SHOPPING LIST**

- Spare ribs (one rack)
- 1 apple's juice
- 2 jalapeños peppers cut in half, deseeded
- tablespoons of chilli (in powder)
- 2 tablespoons of ground cumin
- 2 tablespoons of salt
- Black pepper to taste
- 1 tablespoon of garlic (minced)
- 1 tablespoon of dried oregano
- 1 teaspoon of celery seeds and dry thyme
- 1/2 cup of beer
- 1/2 cup of onion, chopped
- 1/4 cup of dry cherries
- 3 tablespoon of BBQ sauce
- 1 tablespoon of olive oil
- 1 garlic glove

🛍️ **DIRECTIONS**

1. Get a bowl and mix oregano, salt, cumin, grated garlic black pepper, celery seeds, chilli powder, thyme. Mix with a food processor.
2. Put the rib on some aluminium foil and rub the mix all over them.
3. Get the apple juice and add it on the ribs then close the foil into a package. Leave to marinate overnight.
4. Put them on the grill around 5 inches away from the wood pellet (better if Maple).
5. Put the jalapenos on a tray and leave them 7 minutes under the preheated broiler.
6. Once cooked peel the skin off.
7. Blend them with onion, beer and cherries. Add some oil and pepper.
8. Put the ribs in the oven at 200 F for 3-4 hours.
9. Then smoke for 1 hour at 250 F
10. Take the foil and the remaining apple juice away and let the ribs cooked in the smoker for 10 mins or until the surface dries out.
11. Brush with the salsa and cook for another 15 mins per side.

Tender Pulled Pork

📖 NUTRITION

Calories: 220
Fat: 15 g
Carbs: 1 g
Protein: 20 g
Fiber: 0 g

📖 INTOLERANCES:

Gluten-Free
Egg-Free

12 | 10 MINUTES

9 HOURS

🧺 SHOPPING LIST

- 9 pounds pork shoulder, bone-in, fat trimmed
- BBQ rub as needed and more as required
- 2 cups apple cider

📋 DIRECTIONS

1. Switch on the Smoker grill, fill the grill hopper with apple-flavored wood pellets, power the grill on by using the control panel, select 'smoke' on the temperature dial, or set the temperature to 250 degrees F and let it preheat for a minimum of 15 minutes.
2. Meanwhile, prepare the pork shoulder, and for this, season it generously with game rub until well coated.
3. When the grill has preheated, open the lid, place pork should on the grill grate fat-side up, shut the grill and smoke for 5 hours, and then remove pork from the grill.
4. Take a large baking sheet, line it with 4 large aluminum foil pieces to wrap pork, place pork in the center, bring up the sides of the foil, pour in apple cider, and then wrap tightly.
5. Transfer baking sheet containing wrapped pork on the grill grate and then cook for 4 hours until the internal temperature reaches to 204 degrees F.
6. When done, remove the baking sheet from the grill, let it rest for 45 minutes, then uncover it, place the pork into a large dish and drain excess liquid into a bowl.
7. Shred pork by using two forks, remove and discard excess fat and bone, then drizzle with reserved liquid and season with some rub.
8. Serve straight away.

Traditional Pork Steak

📖 NUTRITION

Calories: 250 Cal

Fat: 21 g

Carbs: 1 g

Protein: 17 g

📖 INTOLERANCES:

Gluten-Free

Egg-Free

4 | 10 MINUTES

20 MINUTES

🧺 SHOPPING LIST

- 2-inch piece of orange peel
- 2 sprigs of thyme
- 4 tablespoons salt
- 4 black peppercorns
- 1 sprig of rosemary
- 2 tablespoons brown sugar
- 2 bay leaves
- 10 cups water
- 4 pork steaks, fat trimmed
- BBQ rub as needed

🛍 DIRECTIONS

1. Prepare the brine and for this, take a large container, place all of its ingredients in it and stir until sugar has dissolved.
2. Place all the steaks in it, add some weights to keep steak submerge into the brine and let soak overnight.
3. The next day, when ready to cook, switch on the grill, fill the grill hopper with hickory flavored wood pellets, power the grill on by using the control panel, select 'smoke' on the temperature dial, or set the temperature to 225 degrees F and let it preheat for a minimum of 15 minutes.
4. Meanwhile, remove all the steaks from the brine, rinse well, pat dry with paper towels and then season well with game rub until coated.

5. When the grill has preheated, open the lid, place steaks on the grill grate, shut the grill and smoke for 10 minutes per side until the internal temperature reaches the 140 degrees F.
6. When done, transfer the steaks to a cutting board, let them rest for 10 minutes, then cut into slices and serve.

Bacon-Wrapped Sausages in Brown Sugar

📖 NUTRITION

Calories: 270 Cal, Fat: 27 g, Carbs: 18 g, Protein: 9 g, Fiber: 2 g

6 | 20 MINUTES

30 MINUTES

📖 INTOLERANCES

Gluten-Free
Egg-Free

🧺 SHOPPING LIST

- 1 pound bacon strips, halved
- 14 ounces cocktail sausages
- ½ cup brown sugar

🛍 DIRECTIONS

1. Place bacon strips on clean working space, roll them by using a rolling pin, and then wrap a sausage with a bacon strip, securing with a toothpick.
2. Place wrapped sausage in a casserole dish, repeat with the other sausages, place them into the casserole dish in a single layer, cover with sugar and then let them sit for 30 minutes in the refrigerator.
3. When ready to cook, switch on the grill, fill the grill hopper with apple-flavored wood pellets, power the grill on by using the control panel, select 'smoke' on the temperature dial, or set the temperature to 350 degrees F and let it preheat for a minimum of 15 minutes.
4. Meanwhile, remove the casserole dish from the refrigerator and then arrange sausage on a cookie sheet lined with parchment paper.
5. When the grill has preheated, open the lid, place cookie sheet on the grill grate, shut the grill and smoke for 30 minutes.
6. When done, transfer sausages to a dish and then serve.

Sweet and Hot BBQ Ribs

 NUTRITION

Calories: 250.8 Cal, Fat: 16.3 g,
Carbs: 6.5 g, Protein: 18.2 g,
Fiber: 0.2 g

INTOLERANCES:

Gluten-Free
Egg-Free

8 · **20 MINUTES**

5 HOURS

 SHOPPING LIST

- 2 racks of pork ribs, bone-in, membrane removed
- 6 ounces pork and poultry rub
- 8 ounces apple juice
- 16 ounces sweet and heat BBQ sauce

DIRECTIONS

1. Sprinkle pork and poultry rub on all sides of pork ribs until evenly coated, rub well and marinate for a minimum of 30 minutes.
2. When ready to cook, switch on the Smoker grill, fill the grill hopper with pecan flavored wood pellets, power the grill on by using the control panel, select 'smoke' on the temperature dial, or set the temperature to 225 degrees F and let it preheat for a minimum of 15 minutes.
3. When the grill has preheated, open the lid, place pork ribs on the grill grate bone-side down, shut the grill and smoke for 1 hour, spraying with 10 ounces of apple juice frequently.
4. Then wrap ribs in aluminum foil, pour in remaining 6 ounces of apple juice,

and wrap tightly.
5. Return wrapped ribs onto the grill grate meat-side down, shut the grill and smoke for 3 to 4 hours until internal temperature reaches 203 degrees F.
6. Remove wrapped ribs from the grill, uncover it and then brush well with the sauce.
7. Return pork ribs onto the grill grate and then grill for 10 minutes until glazed.
8. When done, transfer ribs to a cutting board, let rest for 10 minutes, then cut it into slices and serve.

Grilled Carnitas

📖 NUTRITION

Calories: 514, Fat: 41.1g,
Cholesterol: 134mg,
Carbohydrate: 1.6g, Protein: 32g

📖 INTOLERANCES:

Gluten-Free
Egg-Free
Lactose-Free

12

🧺 SHOPPING LIST

- 1 tsp paprika
- 1 tsp oregano
- 1 tsp cayenne pepper
- 2 tsp brown sugar
- 1 tsp mint
- 1 tbsp onion powder
- 1 tsp cumin
- 1 tsp chili powder
- 2 tbsp salt
- 1 tsp garlic powder
- 1 tsp Italian seasoning
- 2 tbsp olive oil.
- 5 pounds pork shoulder roast

🛍 DIRECTIONS

1. Trim the pork of any excess fat.
2. To make rub, combine the paprika, oregano, cayenne, sugar, mint, onion powder, garlic powder, cumin, chili, salt, and Italian seasoning in a small mixing bowl.
3. Rub all sides of the pork with the rub.
4. Start your grill for smoking, leaving the lid open until fire starts.
5. Close the lid and preheat grill to 325°F with lid closed for 15 minutes.
6. Place the pork in a foil pan and place the pan on the grill—Cook for about 2 hours.
7. After 2 hours, increase the heat to 325°F and smoke pork for an additional 8 hours or until the pork's internal temperature reaches 190°F.
8. Remove pork from it and let it sit until it is cook and easy to handle.
9. Shred the pork with two forks.
10. Place a cast-iron skillet on the grill grate and add the olive oil.
11. Add the pork and sear until the pork is brown and crispy.
12. Remove pork from heat and let it rest for a few minutes.
13. Serve.

20 MINUTES

10 HOUR

Stuffed Tenderloin

NUTRITION

Calories: 241, Fat: 14.8g,
Cholesterol: 66mg,
Carbohydrate: 2.7g, Protein: 22.9g

INTOLERANCES:

Gluten-Free
Egg-Free

15 MINUTES

3 HOUR

8

SHOPPING LIST

- 1 pork tenderloin
- 12 slices of bacon
- ¼ cup cheddar cheese
- ¼ cup mozzarella cheese
- 1 small onion (finely chopped)
- 1 carrot (finely chopped)
- Rub:
- ½ tsp granulated garlic (not garlic powder)
- ½ tsp cayenne pepper
- 1 tsp paprika
- ½ tsp ground pepper
- 1 tsp chili
- ½ tsp onion powder
- ¼ tsp cumin
- 1 tsp salt

DIRECTIONS

1. Butterfly the pork tenderloin and place between 2 plastic wraps. Pound the tenderloin evenly with a mallet until it is ½ inch thick.
2. Place the cheddar, mozzarella, onion, and carrot on one end of the flat pork. Roll up the pork like a burrito.
3. Combine all the ingredients for the rub in a mixing bowl. Rub the seasoning mixture all over the pork.
4. Wrap the pork with bacon slices.
5. Preheat the grill to 275°F for 10-15 minutes. Use apple, hickory, or mesquite hardwood pellets.
6. Place the pork on the grill and smoke for 3 hours, or until the pork's internal temperature reaches 165°F and the bacon wrap is crispy.
7. Remove the pork from heat and let it rest for about 10 minutes.
8. Cut into sizes and serve.

Pork Kebabs

 **NUTRITION**

Calories: 272, Fat: 15.8g,
Cholesterol: 62mg,
Carbohydrate: 9.2g, Protein: 24g

 **INTOLERANCES:**

Gluten-Free
Egg-Free
Lactose-Free

 20 MINUTES

 10 MINUTES

 4

 SHOPPING LIST

- 1 pork tenderloin (cut into 2-inch cubes)
- 1 large bell pepper (sliced)
- 1 large yellow bell pepper (sliced)
- 1 large green bell pepper (sliced)
- 1 onion (sliced)
- 10 medium cremini mushrooms (destemmed and halved)
- Wooden or bamboo skewers (soaked in water for 30 minutes, at least)

Marinade:
- ½ cup olive oil
- ½ tsp pepper
- 1 tsp salt
- 1 tbsp freshly chopped parsley
- 3 tbsp brown sugar
- 2 tsp Dijon mustard
- 3 tbsp soy sauce
- 1 lemon (juice)
- 1 tbsp freshly chopped thyme
- 1 tsp minced garlic

DIRECTIONS

1. In a large mixing bowl, combine all the marinade ingredients. Add the pork and mushroom. Toss to combine. Cover the bowl tightly with aluminum foil and refrigerate for 8 hours.
2. Remove the mushroom and pork from the marinade.
3. Thread the bell peppers, onion, mushroom and pork onto skewers to make kabobs.
4. Preheat your grill to high with lid closed for 15 minutes, using mesquite hardwood pellets.
5. Arrange the kebobs onto the grill grate and grill for 12 minutes, 6 minutes per side, or until the pork's internal temperature reaches 145°F.
6. Remove kebabs from heat.

Maplewood Bourbon BBQ Ham

NUTRITION

Calories: 163, Fat: 4.6g,
Cholesterol: 29mg,
Carbohydrate: 19g, Protein: 8.7g

INTOLERANCES:

Gluten-Free
Egg-Free
Lactose-Free

 15 MINUTES

 2 HOURS 30 MINUTES

SHOPPING LIST

- 1 large ham
- 1/2 cup brown sugar
- 3 tbsp bourbon
- 2 tbsp lemon
- 2 tbsp Dijon mustard
- ¼ cup apple juice
- ¼ cup maple syrup
- 1 tsp salt
- 1 tsp freshly ground garlic
- 1 tsp ground black pepper

DIRECTIONS

1. Start your grill on smoke setting, leaving for 5 minutes, until fire starts.
2. Close the lid and preheat grill to 325°F.
3. Place the ham on a smoker rack and place the rack on the grill. Smoke for 2 hours or until the internal temperature of the ham reaches 125°F.
4. Combine the sugar, bourbon, lemon, mustard, apple juice, salt, pepper, and maple in a saucepan over medium to high heat.
5. Bring mixture to a boil, reduce the heat and simmer until the sauce thickens.
6. Glaze the ham with maple mixture.
7. Increase the grill temperature to 375°F and continue cooking until the internal temperature of the ham reaches 140°F.
8. Remove the glazed ham from the grill and let it rest for about 15 minutes.
9. Cut ham into small sizes and serve.

 8

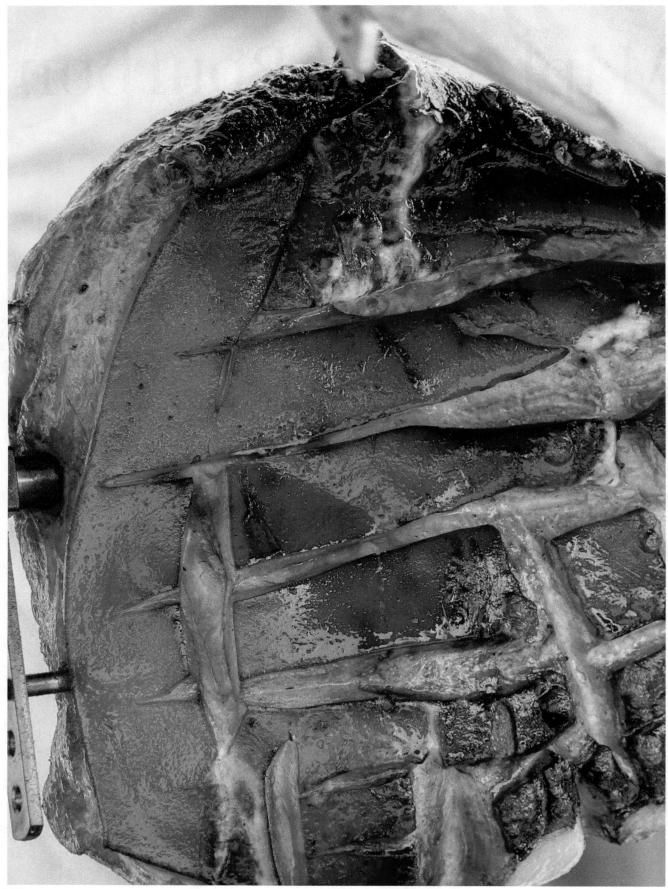

Southern Grilled Pork Chops

NUTRITION

Calories: 216, Fat: 12g,
Cholesterol: 76mg,
Carbohydrate: 3g, Protein: 25.3g

INTOLERANCES:

Gluten-Free
Egg-Free
Lactose-Free

SHOPPING LIST

- 4 center cut boneless pork chops
- 2 tbsp olive oil

Rub:
- 1 tsp kosher salt or to taste
- 1 tsp Italian seasoning
- 1 tsp Greek seasoning
- ½ tsp cayenne pepper
- 2 tsp brown sugar
- 1 tsp finely chopped fresh rosemary
- 1 tsp ground black pepper
- 1 tsp dried basil
- ½ tsp peppermint
- ½ tsp oregano
- ½ tsp ground cumin

DIRECTIONS

1. Start your grill on smoke mode, leaving the lid open until fire starts.
2. Preheat grill to 180°F, using hickory hardwood pellet.
3. Combine all the ingredients for the rub ingredients in a small mixing bowl.
4. Drizzle all sides of the pork chops with oil. Liberally season all sides of each pork chop with the rub.
5. Place the pork chops on the grill and smoke, with lid closed, for 45 minutes.
6. Remove the pork chops from the grill and preheat the grill to 450°F.
7. Return the pork chops to the grill and smoke for 20 minutes or until the pork chops' internal temperature reaches 150°F.
8. Remove the pork chop from the grill and let it rest for about 15 minutes.
9. Slice and serve.

15 MINUTES

1 HOUR

4

Porchetta

 SHOPPING LIST

- 6 pounds skin-on pork belly
- 4 pounds center cut pork loin
- 4 tbsp olive oil
- 1 cup apple juice
- 2 garlic cloves (minced)
- 1 onion (diced)
- 1 ¼ cups grated pecorino Romano cheese
- 1 tsp ground black pepper
- 2 tsp kosher salt - 3 tbsp fennel seeds
- 1 tbsp freshly chopped rosemary
- 1 tbsp freshly chopped sage
- 1 tbsp freshly chopped thyme
- 1 tbsp grated lemon zest
- Rub:
- 1 tbsp chili powder - 2 tsp grilling seasoning
- 1 tsp salt or to taste
- ½ tsp cayenne
- 1 tsp oregano - 1 tsp paprika
- 1 tsp mustard powder

- Butterfly the pork loin and place it in the middle of two plastic wraps. On a flat surface, pound the pork evenly until it is ½ inch thick.
- Combine all the rub ingredients in a small mixing bowl.
- Place the butterflied pork on a flat surface, cut side up. Season the cut side generously with 1/3 of the rub.
- Heat 1 tbsp olive oil in a frying pan over medium to high heat. Add the onion, garlic and fennel seed. Sauté until the veggies are tender.
- Stir the black pepper, 1 tsp kosher salt, rosemary, sage, thyme and lemon zest. Cook for 1 minutes and stir in the cheese.
- Put the sautéed ingredients on the flat pork and spread evenly. Roll up the pork like you are rolling a burrito.
- Brush the rolled pork loin with 1 tbsp oil and season with the remaining rub. The loin with butcher's string at 1-inch interval.

- Roll the pork belly around the pork, skin side out. Brush the pork belly with the remaining oil and season with 1 tsp salt.
- Set a rack into a roasting pan and place the Porchetta on the rack. Pour the wine into the bottom of the roasting pan.
- Start your grill on smoke mode, leaving the lid opened for 5 minutes until fire starts.
- Close the lid and preheat grill to 325°F, using maple or apple hardwood pellets.
- Place the roasting pan on the grill and roast Porchetta for about 3 hours or until the Porchetta's internal temperature reaches 155°F.
- Remove the Porchetta from heat and let it rest for a few minutes to cool.
- Remove the butcher's string. Slice Porchetta into sizes and serve.

Pork Jerky

NUTRITION

Calories: 260, Fat: 11.4g,
Cholesterol: 80mg,
Carbohydrate: 8.6g, Protein: 28.1g

INTOLERANCES:

Gluten-Free
Egg-Free
Lactose-Free

2 HR 30 MINUTES

12

SHOPPING LIST

- 4 pounds boneless center cut pork (trimmed of excess fat and sliced into ¼ inch thick slices)
  Marinade:
- 1/3 cup soy sauce
- 1 cup pineapple juice
- 1 tbsp rice wine vinegar
- 2 tsp black pepper
- 1 tsp red pepper

- flakes
- 5 tbsp brown sugar
- 1 tsp paprika
- 1 tsp onion powder
- 1 tsp garlic powder
- 2 tsp salt or to taste

DIRECTIONS

1. Combine and mix all the marinade ingredients in a mixing bowl.
2. Put the sliced pork in a gallon-sized zip-lock bag and pour the marinade into the bag. Massage the marinade into the pork. Seal the bag and refrigerate for 8 hours.
3. Activate the pellet grill smoker setting and leave lip open for 5 minutes until fire starts.
4. Close the lid and preheat your pellet grill to 180°F, using hickory pellet.
5. Remove the pork slices from the marinade and pat them dry with a paper towel.
6. Arrange the pork slices on the grill in a single layer. Smoke the pork for about 2 ½ hours, turning often after the first 1 hour of smoking. The jerky should be dark and dry when it is done.
7. Remove the jerky from the grill and let it sit for about 1 hour to cool.
8. Serve immediately or store in airtight containers and refrigerate for future use.

Lemon Pepper Pork Tenderloin

NUTRITION

Calories: 289, Fat: 17g,
Carbs: 6.2g,
Protein: 26.5g

INTOLERANCES:

Gluten-Free
Egg-Free
Lactose-Free

20 MINUTES

20 MINUTES

SHOPPING LIST

- 2 pounds pork tenderloin, fat trimmed

For the Marinade:
- ½ teaspoon minced

- garlic
- 2 lemons, zested
- 1 teaspoon minced parsley
- 1/2 teaspoon salt

- 1/4 teaspoon ground black pepper
- 1 teaspoon lemon juice
- 2 tablespoons olive oil

DIRECTIONS

1. To prepare the marinade, take a small bowl, place all ingredients in it and whisk until combined.
2. Take a large plastic bag, pour marinade in it, add pork tenderloin, seal the bag, turn it upside down to coat the pork and let it marinate for a minimum of 2 hours in the refrigerator.
3. Fill the grill hopper with apple-flavored wood pellets, power the grill on by using the control panel, select 'smoke' on the temperature dial, or set the temperature to 375°F and let it preheat for a minimum of 15 minutes.
4. When the grill has preheated, open the lid, place pork tenderloin on the grill grate, shut the grill and smoke for 20 minutes until internal temperature reaches 145°F, make sure to turn pork halfway.
5. When done, transfer the pork to a cutting board, let it rest for 10 minutes, then cut it into slices and serve.

6

Chinese BBQ Pork

NUTRITION

Calories: 281, Fat: 8g,
Carbs: 13g, Protein: 40g

INTOLERANCES:

Gluten-Free

Egg-Free

Lactose-Free

SHOPPING LIST

- 2 pork tenderloins, silver skin removed
For the Marinade:
- ½ teaspoon minced garlic
- 1 1/2 tablespoon brown sugar
- 1 teaspoon Chinese five-spice

- 1/4 cup honey
- 1 tablespoon Asian sesame oil
- 1/4 cup hoisin sauce
- 2 teaspoons red food coloring
- 1 tablespoon oyster sauce, optional
- 3 tablespoons soy

sauce
For the Five-Spice Sauce:
- 1/4 teaspoon Chinese five-spice
- 3 tablespoons brown sugar
- 1 teaspoon yellow mustard
- 1/4 cup ketchup

DIRECTIONS

1. Prepare the marinade and for this, take a small bowl, place all ingredients in it and whisk until combined.
2. Take a large plastic bag, pour marinade in it, add pork tenderloin, seal the bag, turn it upside down to coat the pork and let it marinate for a minimum of 8 hours in the refrigerator.
3. Fill the grill hopper with maple-flavored wood pellets, power the grill on by using the control panel, select 'smoke' on the temperature

dial, or set the temperature to 225°F and let it preheat for a minimum of 5 minutes.
4. Remove pork from the marinade, transfer marinade into a small saucepan, place it over medium-high heat and cook for 3 minutes, and then set aside until cooled.
5. When the grill has preheated, open the lid, place pork on the grill grate, shut the grill and smoke for 2 hours, basting with the marinade halfway.
6. Prepare the five-spice sauce and for this, take a small saucepan, place

it over low heat, add all ingredients, stir until well combined and sugar has dissolved and cooked for 5 minutes until hot and thickened, set aside until required.

7. When done, transfer pork to a dish, let rest for 15 minutes, and meanwhile, change the smoking temperature of the grill to 450°F and let it preheat for a minimum of 10 minutes.
8. Return pork to the grill grate and cook for 3 minutes per side until slightly charred.
9. Transfer pork to a dish, let rest for 5 minutes, and then serve with prepared five-spice sauce.

Smoked Sausages

 NUTRITION

Calories: 231, Fat: 22 g,
Carbs: 2 g, Protein: 15 g

 INTOLERANCES:

Gluten-Free

Egg-Free

Lactose-Free

 15 MINUTES

 3 HOURS

 4

 SHOPPING LIST

- 3 pounds ground pork
- 1 tablespoon onion powder
- 1 tablespoon garlic
- powder
- 1 teaspoon curing salt
- 4 teaspoon black pepper
- 1/2 tablespoon salt
- 1/2 tablespoon ground mustard
- Hog casings, soaked
- 1/2 cup ice water

DIRECTIONS

1. Fill the grill hopper with flavored wood pellets, power the grill on by using the control panel, select 'smoke' on the temperature dial, or set the temperature to 225°F and let it preheat for a minimum of 15 minutes.
2. Take a medium bowl, place all the ingredients in it except for water and hog casings, and stir until well mixed.
3. Pour in water, stir until incorporated, place the mixture in a sausage stuffer, then stuff the hog casings and tie the link to the desired length.
4. When the grill has preheated, open the lid, place the sausage links on the grill grate, shut the grill, and smoke for 2 to 3 hours until the

internal temperature reaches 155°F.
5. Transfer sausages to a dish, let them rest for 5 minutes, then slice and serve.

Grilled Pork Belly

📖 NUTRITION

Calories: 431, Fat: 45g,
Carbs: 1g, Protein: 8g

📖 INTOLERANCES:

Gluten-Free
Egg-Free
Lactose-Free

10 MINUTES

3 HR 30 MINUTES

6

🧺 SHOPPING LIST

- 3 pounds pork belly, skin removed
- Pork and poultry rub as needed
- 4 tablespoons salt
- 1/2 teaspoon ground black pepper

🛍 DIRECTIONS

1. Fill the grill hopper with apple-flavored wood pellets, power the grill on by using the control panel, select 'smoke' on the temperature dial, or set the temperature to 275°F and let it preheat for a minimum of 15 minutes.
2. Prepare the pork belly and for this, sprinkle pork and poultry rub, salt, and black pepper on all sides of pork belly until well coated.
3. When the grill has preheated, open the lid, place the pork belly on the grill grate, shut the grill and smoke for 3 hours and 30 minutes until the internal temperature reaches 200°F.
4. Transfer pork belly to a cutting board, let it rest for 15 minutes, then cut it into slices and serve.

Oregano Pork Tenderloin

NUTRITION

Calories: 267, Fat: 18g,
Carbs: 3g, Protein: 16g

INTOLERANCES:

Gluten-Free
Egg-Free
Lactose-Free

SHOPPING LIST

- 2 pounds pork tenderloin, fat trimmed

For the Marinade:
- ½ teaspoon minced garlic
- 1 tbsp. of Oregano
- 1 teaspoon minced parsley
- 1/2 teaspoon salt
- 1/4 teaspoon ground black pepper
- 2 tbsp. soy sauce
- 2 tablespoons olive oil

DIRECTIONS

1. Prepare the marinade and for this, take a small bowl, place all of its ingredients in it and whisk until combined.
2. Take a large plastic bag, pour marinade in it, add pork tenderloin, seal the bag, turn it upside down to coat the pork and let it marinate for a minimum of 2 hours in the refrigerator.
3. When ready to cook, switch on the Traeger grill, fill the grill hopper with apple-flavored wood pellets, power the grill on by using the control panel, select 'smoke' on the temperature dial, or set the temperature to 375 degrees F and let it preheat for a minimum of 15 minutes.
4. When the grill has preheated, open the lid, place pork tenderloin on the grill grate, shut the grill and smoke for 20 minutes until internal temperature reaches 145 degrees F, turning pork halfway.
5. When done, transfer pork to a cutting board, let it rest for 10 minutes, then cut it into slices and serve.

20 MINUTES · 20 MINUTES · 6

BBQ Hot Dogs

NUTRITION

Calories: 50, Protein: 1g
Carbs: 3g, Fat: 4g

INTOLERANCES

Gluten-Free
Egg-Free
Lactose-Free

SHOPPING LIST

- 3 pounds ground pork
- 1 tablespoon onion powder
- 1 tablespoon garlic powder
- 1 teaspoon curing salt
- 4 teaspoon black pepper
- 1/2 tablespoon salt
- 1/2 tablespoon ground mustard
- Hog casings, soaked
- 1/2 cup ice water

DIRECTIONS

1. Switch on the smoker grill, fill the grill hopper with flavored wood pellets, power the grill on by using the control panel, select 'smoke' on the temperature dial, or set the temperature to 225 degrees F and let it preheat for a minimum of 15 minutes.
2. Meanwhile, take a medium bowl, place all the ingredients in it except for water and hog casings, and stir until well mixed.
3. Pour in water, stir until incorporated, place the mixture in a sausage stuffer, then stuff the hog casings and tie the link to the desired length.
4. When the grill has preheated, open the lid, place the sausage links on the grill grate, shut the grill, and smoke for 2 to 3 hours until the internal temperature reaches 155 degrees F.
5. When done, transfer sausages to a dish, let them rest for 5 minutes, then slice and serve.

15 MINUTES | 2 - 3 HOURS | 4

BBQ Baby Back Ribs

 **NUTRITION**

Calories: 334 Cal, Fat: 23 g,
Carbs: 6.7 g, Protein: 24 g,
Fiber: 0.2 g

 **INTOLERANCES:**

Gluten-Free

Egg-Free

8   15 MINUTES   6H

 SHOPPING LIST

- 2 racks of baby back pork ribs, membrane removed
- Pork and poultry rub as needed
- 1/2 cup brown sugar
- 1/3 cup honey, warmed
- 1/3 cup yellow mustard
- 1 tablespoon
- Worcestershire sauce
- 1 cup BBQ sauce
- 1/2 cup apple juice, divided

 DIRECTIONS

1. Switch on the Smoker grill, fill the grill hopper with hickory flavored wood pellets, power the grill on by using the control panel, select 'smoke' on the temperature dial, or set the temperature to 180 degrees F and let it preheat for a minimum of 15 minutes.
2. Meanwhile, take a small bowl, place mustard, and Worcestershire sauce in it, pour in ¼ cup apple juice and whisk until combined and smooth paste comes together.
3. Brush this paste on all sides of ribs and then season with pork and poultry rub until coated.
4. When the grill has preheated, open the lid, place ribs on the grill grate meat-side up, shut the grill and smoke for 3 hours.
5. After 3 hours, transfer ribs to a rimmed baking dish, let rest for 15 minutes, and meanwhile, change the smoking temperature of the grill to 225 degrees F and let it preheat for a minimum of 10 minutes.
6. Then return pork into the rimmed baking sheet to the grill grate and cook for 3 minutes per side until slightly charred.
7. When done, remove the baking sheet from the grill and work on one rib at a time, sprinkle half of the sugar over the rib, drizzle with half of the honey and half of the remaining apple juice, cover with aluminum foil to seal completely.
8. Repeat with the remaining ribs, return foiled ribs on the grill grate, shut with lid, and then smoke for 2 hours.
9. After 2 hours, uncover the grill, brush them with BBQ sauce generously, arrange them on the grill grate and grill for 1 hour until glazed.
10. When done, transfer ribs to a cutting board, let it rest for 15 minutes, slice into pieces and then serve.

CHAPTER 8

Fish and Seafood Recipes

Spicy Marinated Tuna Steak

 NUTRITION

Calories: 270, Fat: 22g,
Cholesterol: 11mg,
Carbs: 2g, Protein: 20g

 DIRECTIONS

1. Take a big non-reactive dish and merge soy sauce, lemon juice, oregano, orange juice, parsley, pepper, garlic, olive oil, and pepper.
2. First, preheat the grill for elevated heat and lightly oil the grate. Cook the tuna steak for five to six minutes and then discard leftover marinade.
3. Additional tip
4. You can serve this dish with leftover cilantro.

 INTOLERANCES

Gluten-Free
Egg-Free

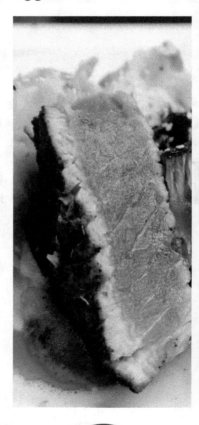

 **SHOPPING LIST**

- ¼ cup of orange juice
- ¼ cup of soy sauce
- Two tablespoons olive oil
- One clove garlic, minced
- Half teaspoon chopped fresh oregano
- Half teaspoon ground black pepper
- One tablespoon lemon juice
- Two tablespoons chopped fresh parsley
- Four tuna steaks

10 MINUTES

12 MINUTES

4

Grilled Salmon

 NUTRITION

Calories: 290, Fat: 14g,
Cholesterol: 80g, Carbs: 1g,
Protein: 38g

 INTOLERANCES

Gluten-Free

Egg-Free

 DIRECTIONS

 15 MINUTES

 30 MINUTES

1. Take a deep glass baking dish and merge orange juice concentrate, mustard, tomato sauce, soy sauce, green onion, ginger, lemon juice, oil, and garlic.
2. Put salmon in the marinade and turn it and cover it, keep in the freezer for a half -hour to one hour.
3. Now, preheat the grill for elevate heat.
4. Eliminate the salmon from the marinade. Pour the marinade in the little saucepan. Allow to boil and cook for one minute.
5. Now, lightly oil the grill grate and brush or sprinkle salmon with olive oil. Cook on the grill for five to ten minutes until it fish flakes with the fork.
6. Now turn the salmon and brush with boiled marinade halfway.
7. You can cook on the barbecue for five to ten minutes until fish easily flakes with the help of fork.

SHOPPING LIST

- ⅓ Cup soy sauce
- ¼ cup orange juice concentrate
- Two tablespoons vegetable oil
- Two tablespoons tomato sauce
- One clove garlic
- Half teaspoon minced fresh ginger root
- One teaspoon lemon juice
- Four steaks salmon steaks
- One tablespoon olive oil
- Half teaspoon prepared mustard
- One tablespoon green onion, minced

Alternative Halibut Soft Tacos

 NUTRITION

Calories: 30, Fat: 1g,
Cholesterol: 17mg,
Carbs: 1g
Protein: 6g

 INTOLERANCES

Gluten-Free
Egg-Free
Lactose-Free

 **SHOPPING LIST**

- 1 mango, diced
- Half cup diced avocado
- ¼ cup chopped red onion
- 2 medium tomatoes, chopped
- 2 medium jalapeno peppers
- 1 teaspoon olive oil
- Half tsp. salt
- 2 tsp. olive oil
- 2 tbsp. minced fresh parsley
- 1 pound halibut steaks
- 1 tsp. lemon juice
- 1 tsp. honey
- ¼ tsp. ground black pepper
- ¼ teaspoon garlic salt
- 4 large leaves Bibb lettuce leaves
- 4 flour tortillas
- 4 teaspoons taco sauce

 DIRECTIONS

1. First, preheat the grill for high flame and softly oil the grate.
2. Blend avocado, mango, parsley, tomatoes, onion, two tablespoon olive oil, honey, jalapeno pepper, and lemon juice in the little bowl.
3. Brush halibut steaks with one tablespoon olive oil and season with garlic salt, salt, and black pepper.
4. Keep halibut on the grill and cover the lid and cook until it gets flakes easily with the help of a fork for three to five minutes.
5. Keep Bibb lettuce leaves on the top of every tortilla. Split halibut into four parts and then nestle in the lettuce leaves.
6. Top with the mixture of mango and sprinkle with taco sauce
7. Additional Tip: To cook the halibut brush the fillets with olive oil and sprinkle with pepper and salt.

4 | 25 MINUTES | 5 MINUTES

South American Grouper

NUTRITION

Calories: 230, Fat: 10g,
Carbs: 1g, Protein: 30g

INTOLERANCES:

Gluten-Free
Egg-Free
Lactose-Free

12 MINUTES

4

20 MINUTES

SHOPPING LIST

- Four grouper fillets
- ⅓ Cup tequila
- Half cup orange liqueur
- ¾ cup fresh lime juice
- Four tablespoons olive oil
- One teaspoon salt
- Three large cloves garlic
- One normal sized jalapeno, seeded and minced
- 3 intermediate tomatoes
- One medium onion
- 4 tablespoons chopped fresh cilantro
- 1 tsp. olive oil
- 1 tsp. ground black pepper
- 11 pinch white sugar
- One teaspoon salt

DIRECTIONS

1. Put fish in the deep baking dish. Take a bowl and stir lime juice, garlic, tequila, one teaspoon salt, garlic, Orange liqueur, and olive oil.
2. Pour the mixture over the fillets and then rub in the fish. Coat and keep in the freezer for half an hour and then turning fillets for one time.
3. After, preheat the grill for high temperature.
4. Take an intermediate bowl and then toss onion, cilantro, sugar, tomatoes, and jalapeno and then season with salt and keep salsa aside.
5. Eliminate the fillets from the marinade and then dry them. Brush the fillets with oil and drizzle with ground black pepper. Take a little saucepan and boil the marinade for few a minutes.
6. Now, eliminate from the flame and then strain out the garlic cloves. Keep aside to chill.
7. Now, Grill fish for four minutes each side until fish gets flaked with the help of a fork
8. Move fillets to many dishes. Move the fish to plate and spoon salsa over the fish and sprinkle with cooked marinade for serving .

Grilled Oyster

 NUTRITION

Calories: 140, Fat: 5g,
Cholesterol: 46mg,
Carbs: 4g, Protein: 20g

 **INTOLERANCES:**

Gluten-Free
Egg-Free

5 MINUTES

10 MINUTES

 SHOPPING LIST

- 8 medium fresh oysters in shells
- ⅓ cup Fresh lemon juice
- 1 dash hot pepper sauce to taste
- 1 pinch salt
- 3 tablespoons Worcestershire sauce

4

DIRECTIONS

1. First, preheat the grill for elevated heat and collect all ingredients.
2. Put the whole oyster on the warm grill and cook until it gets open for five to ten minutes.
3. Eliminate the oyster from the grill and snoop the shell top. Slide a sharp knife among the shell and oyster to separate.
4. Top each with salt, one tablespoon Worcestershire sauce, two tablespoon lemon juice, and warm pepper sauce.
5. Serve in the shell while still hot.

Tasty Grilled Shrimp

NUTRITION

Calories: 230, Fat: 10g,
Carbs: 1g, Protein: 30g

INTOLERANCES:

Gluten-Free
Egg-Free
Lactose-Free

6 MINUTES

6

15 MINUTES

SHOPPING LIST

- One large clove garlic
- One teaspoon coarse salt
- Two tablespoons olive oil

- Two teaspoons lemon juice
- Two pounds large shrimp
- Eight wedges lemon
- Half teaspoon

- cayenne pepper
- One teaspoon paprika

DIRECTIONS

1. First, preheat the grill for intermediate heat.
2. Take a little bowl and grind the garlic with salt. Merge paprika and cayenne pepper and then stir in the lemon juice and olive oil to make a paste.
3. Take a big bowl and toss shrimp with a paste of garlic until it gets coated.
4. Now, lightly oil the grate on the grill.
5. Cook the shrimp for two to three minutes per side until it gets opaque.
6. Move to the serving dish and decorate with lemon wedges and serve
7. Additional tip: Before serving, you can add grilled lemon wedges over the dish

Simple Grilled Salmon with lemon & pepper

NUTRITION

Calories: 140, Fat: 5g,
Cholesterol: 46mg,
Carbs: 4g, Protein: 20g

INTOLERANCES:

Gluten-Free
Egg-Free

15 MINUTES
16 MINUTES

SHOPPING LIST

- One and a half pounds salmon fillet
- Half teaspoon lemon pepper
- ¼ teaspoon garlic powder
- ⅓ Cup brown sugar
- ⅓ Cup water
- ¼ cup of vegetable oil
- Half teaspoon salt to taste
- ⅓ Cup soy sauce

DIRECTIONS

6

1. First, season salmon fillets with salt, lemon pepper, and garlic powder.
2. Take a little bowl and stir brown sugar, vegetable oil, soy sauce, and water until sugar is completely dissolved. Add fish in the big plastic bag with a mixture of soy sauce and seal it and then turn to coat. Keep in the freezer for two hours. Now, preheat the grill for intermediate heat.
3. Now, lightly oil the grate and put salmon on the preheated grill and remove the marinade. Cook salmon for six to eight minutes each side until fish easily flakes with a fork.
4. Additional tip: If you want to store it then keep the lemon pepper salmon in the container suitable for the freezer for one to two days max.

Grilled Shrimps in herbs & garlic

 NUTRITION

Calories: 240, Fat: 15g
Carbs: 25g, Protein: 4g

 INTOLERANCES

Gluten-Free
Egg-Free
Lactose-Free

 **SHOPPING LIST**

- 2 tsp. ground paprika
- 2 tsp. Italian seasoning blend
- Half tsp. ground black pepper
- 2 tsp. of fresh minced garlic
- 2 tsp. of dried basil leaves
- 2 tbsp. of brown sugar, packed
- 2 pounds large shrimp
- 2 tbsp. of fresh lemon juice
- ¼ cup olive oil

 DIRECTIONS

1. First of all take a bowl whisk lemon juice, pepper, Italian seasoning, garlic, brown sugar, olive oil, and basil until blended.
2. After, stir in the shrimp and toss it coat with marinade. Coat and keep in the freezer for two hours, turning for one time.
3. Now, preheat the grill for medium to high heat and lightly oil grill grate and put four inches from the heat source.
4. Eliminate the shrimp from the marinade and drain it and then remove marinade.
5. Keep shrimp on the preheated grill and cook it until it gets opaque in the middle for five to six minutes and serve instantly.
6. Additional tip: Dry the shrimps patting them delicetely before coating with herb puree.

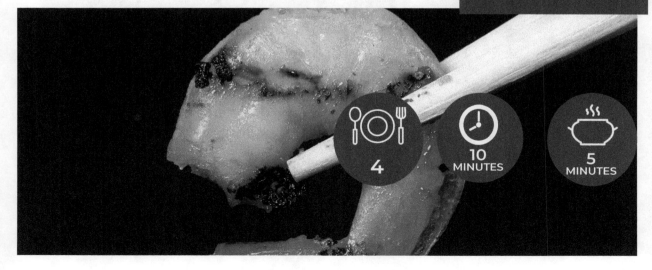

4 | 10 MINUTES | 5 MINUTES

Grilled Cilantro Salmon

 NUTRITION

Calories: 16, Fat: 14g
Carbs: 10g, Protein: 1g

 INTOLERANCES

Gluten-Free
Egg-Free
Lactose-Free

 SHOPPING LIST

- Three pounds salmon
- One fresh jalapeno pepper,
- One teaspoon Old Bay Seasoning TM
- ¼ cup butter
- One cup chopped cilantro

 DIRECTIONS

1. First, preheat the grill for elevated heat. After, lightly grease to 1 side of a big sheet of aluminum foil and put salmon on the greased side of the foil.
2. Take a saucepan and liquefy the butter in the saucepan over intermediate heat. Eliminate from the heat and merge jalapeno and cilantro. Cilantro is wilted and sprinkles the mixture of butter over the salmon.
3. Keep the foil with salmon on the grill and season with old bay.
4. Cook for fifteen minutes until fish easily flakes with the fork.
5. Additional tip: Leave the skin on while grilling the salmon, it'll come off itself.

 10 MINUTES

 20 MINUTES

8

Maui Style Shrimps

 **NUTRITION**

Calories: 9
Carbs: 1g

 INTOLERANCES:

Gluten-Free
Egg-Free
Lactose-Free

15 MINUTES

10 MINUTES

6

 SHOPPING LIST

- Two pounds uncooked medium shrimp, peeled and deveined
- One pinch garlic salt
- One pinch ground black pepper
- ¼ teaspoon cayenne pepper
- One cup mayonnaise
- One lemon, cut into wedges

 DIRECTIONS

1. First, preheat the grill for intermediate heat and lightly oil the grate.
2. After, thread the shrimp on the skewers and season with black pepper and garlic salt
3. Coat equally sides of shrimp with mayonnaise.
4. Fry shrimp on the grilled until shrimp gets bright pink on the outer side and opaque on the inner side, mayonnaise gets golden brown for five to ten minutes on every side. Serve with lemon wedges.
5. Additional tip: You can garnish this dish with popcorn sprouts

Tasty Barbeque Halibut Steaks

 NUTRITION

Calories: 50
Fat: 0.5g
Carbs: 10g
Protein: 1g

INTOLERANCES:

Gluten-Free
Egg-Free
Lactose-Free

15 MINUTES

10 MINUTES

3

SHOPPING LIST

- 2 tbsp. of butter
- 2 tbsp. of brown sugar
- 2 tbsp. of soy sauce
- Half tbsp. ground black pepper
- One halibut steak
- Two cloves garlic, minced
- One tbsp. lemon juice

DIRECTIONS

1. First, preheat the grill for middle to high heat. Add garlic, soy sauce, lemon juice, pepper, brown sugar, and butter in the little saucepan.
2. Heat it and stirring infrequently until the sugar gets completely dissolved.
3. After, lightly oil grill and brush fish with brown sugar sauce and keep on the grill. Cook for five minutes each side until fish easily flakes with a fork and basting with sauce.
4. Remove leftover basting sauce.

Tomatoes and Lime Clams with Grilled Bread

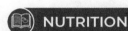

NUTRITION

Calories: 400, Fat: 21g,
Carbs: 33g, Protein: 17g

INTOLERANCES

Gluten-Free
Egg-Free

DIRECTIONS

1. Set up the grill for medium, indirect heat. Put a large skillet on the grill over direct heat and melt 4 tbsp of butter in it.
2. Add the shallots and garlic and keep cooking, often stirring, until they soften, about 4 minutes.
3. Add the tomato paste and keep cooking, continually stirring, until paste darkens to a rich brick red color. Add the beer and tomatoes.
4. Cook until the beer is reduced nearly by half, about 4 minutes. Add in the chickpeas and sambal oelek, then the clams.
5. Cover and keep cooking until clams have opened, maybe from 5 to 10 minutes depending on the size of clams and the heat. Discard any clams that don't open. Pour in the lime juice and the remaining 2 tbsp of butter.
6. While grilling the clams, you can sprinkle the bread with oil and season with salt. Grill until it becomes golden brown and crisp.
7. Put the toasts onto plates and spoon with clam mixture, then top with cilantro. Serve with lime wedges.

25 MINUTES

10 MINUTES

4

SHOPPING LIST

- 6 tbsp unsalted pieces of butter
- 2 large shallots, chopped
- 4 thinly sliced garlic cloves
- 1 tbsp of tomato paste
- 1 cup of beer
- 1 cup cherry tomatoes
- 1 1/2 ounce can-chickpeas, rinsed
- 2 tbsp sambal oelek
- 24 scrubbed littleneck clams
- 1 tbsp fresh lime juice
- 4 thick slices of country-style bread
- 2 tbsp olive oil
- Kosher salt
- ½ cup cilantro leaves
- lime wedges

Grilled Fish with Salsa Verde

 NUTRITION

Calories: 270, Fat: 22g,
Cholesterol: 11mg,
Carbs: 2g, Protein: 20g

 INTOLERANCES

Gluten-Free
Egg-Free

 DIRECTIONS

1. Mix the garlic, orange juice, oregano, one cup onion, ¼ cup cilantro, ¼ cup oil, and 3 tbsp of lime juice in a medium bowl.
2. Season the fish with salt and grounded pepper. Spoon the 1/2 onion mixture on a glass baking dish then put the fish on it.
3. Spoon the remaining onion mixture over the fish and chill for half hour. Turn the fish , cover and chill for another half hour.
4. Mix the mayo, milk, and the remaining two tbsp of lime juice in a little bowl.
5. Set up the grill for medium-high heat and brush the grate with oil.
6. Grill the fish, with some marinade on, till opaque in the center, about 3–5 minutes for each side.
7. Grill the tortillas till slightly burned, about ten seconds per side. Coarsely chop the fish and put it onto a platter.
8. Serve with lime mayonnaise, tortillas, avocados, cabbage, Salsa Verde, lime wedges and the remaining cup of sliced onion and ½ cup cilantro.

SHOPPING LIST

- 2 garlic cloves
- 3 tbsp fresh orange juice
- 1 tsp dried oregano
- 2 cups of chopped white onion
- ¾ cup chopped cilantro
- ¼ cup extra virgin olive oil and more for the grill
- 5 tbsp fresh lime juice
- 1 lb. of tilapia, striped bass or sturgeon fillets
- Kosher salt and grounded pepper
- 1 cup of mayonnaise
- 1 tbsp of milk
- 4 corn tortillas
- 2 avocados, peeled and sliced
- ½ small head of cabbage, cored and thinly sliced
- Salsa Verde
- Lime wedges

4

15 MINUTES

10 MINUTES

Grilled Salmon Steaks with Cilantro Yogurt Sauce

 NUTRITION

Calories: 290, Fat: 14g,
Cholesterol: 80g, Carbs: 1g,
Protein: 38g

 INTOLERANCES

Gluten-Free
Egg-Free

10 MINUTES

10 MINUTES

4

 DIRECTIONS

1. Set up the grill for medium-high heat, then oil the grate.
2. Expel and dispose of seeds from one chili. Mix the two chilis, garlic, cilantro, the yogurt, oil, the nectar, and ¼ cup water in a blender until it becomes smooth, then season well with salt.
3. Move half of the sauce to a little bowl and put it aside. Season the salmon steaks with salt.
4. Grill it, turning more than once, until it's beginning to turn dark, about 4 minutes.
5. Keep on grilling, turning frequently, and seasoning with residual sauce for at least 4 minutes longer.

SHOPPING LIST

- Vegetable oil (for the grill)
- 2 serrano chilis
- 2 garlic cloves
- 1 cup cilantro leaves
- ½ cup plain whole-milk Greek yogurt
- 1 tbsp of extra virgin olive oil
- 1 tsp honey
- Kosher salt
- 2 12oz bone-in salmon steaks

Grilled Scallops in Salsa Verde & Lemon

 NUTRITION

Calories: 30, Fat: 1g,
Cholesterol: 17mg,
Carbs: 1g
Protein: 6g

 INTOLERANCES

Gluten-Free
Egg-Free
Lactose-Free

 **SHOPPING LIST**

- 2 tbsp of vegetable oil and more for the grill
- 12 large sea scallops, side muscle removed
- Kosher salt and grounded black pepper
- Lemony Salsa Verde

DIRECTIONS

1. Set up the grill for medium-high heat, then oil the grate. Toss the scallops with 2 tbsp of oil on a rimmed baking sheet and season with salt and pepper.
2. Utilizing a fish spatula or your hands, place the scallops on the grill.
3. Grill them, occasionally turning, until gently singed and cooked through, around 2 minutes for each side.
4. Serve the scallops with Lemony Salsa Verde.

4 | 15 MINUTES | 5 MINUTES

Grilled Sea Scallops with Corn Salad

NUTRITION

Calories: 230, Fat: 5g
Cholesterol: 60mg,
Carbs: 13g, Protein: 33g

INTOLERANCES

Gluten-Free
Egg-Free
Lactose-Free

DIRECTIONS

1. In a pot of boiling salted water, cook the corn for about 5 minutes. Drain and cool.
2. Place the corn into a big bowl and cut off the kernels. Add the tomatoes, the scallions and basil then season with salt and grounded pepper.
3. In a blender, mix the minced shallot with the vinegar, heated water, and mustard. With the blender on, gradually add 6 tbsp of the sunflower oil.
4. Season the vinaigrette with salt and pepper; at that point, add it to the corn salad.
5. In a huge bowl, toss the remaining 1 tbsp of oil with the scallops, then season with salt and grounded pepper.
6. Heat a grill pan. Put on half of the scallops and grill over high heat, turning once, until singed, around 4 minutes.
7. Repeat with the other half of the scallops. Place the corn salad on plates, then top with the scallops and serve.

SHOPPING LIST

- 6 shucked ears of corn
- 1-pint grape tomatoes, halved
- 3 sliced scallions, white and light green parts only
- 1/3 cup basil leaves, finely shredded
- Salt and grounded pepper
- 1 small shallot, minced
- 2 tbsp balsamic vinegar
- 2 tbsp hot water
- 1 tsp Dijon mustard 1/4 cup
- 3 tbsp sunflower oil
- 1 1/2 pounds sea scallops

25 MINUTES

30 MINUTES

6

Grilled Oysters with Tequila Butter

NUTRITION

Calories: 68, Fat: 3g,
Carbs: 4g, Protein: 10g

INTOLERANCES

Gluten-Free

Egg-Free

Lactose-Free

DIRECTIONS

1. Using a skillet, toast the fennel seeds and squashed red pepper over moderate heat until fragrant for 1 minute.
2. Move onto a mortar and let it cool. With a pestle, pound the spices to a coarse powder, then move into a bowl.
3. Using the same skillet, cook 3 1/2 tbsp of the butter over moderate heat until it becomes dark-colored, about two minutes.
4. Add 1/4 cup of sage and keep cooking, occasionally turning, for about 2 minutes. Move the sage onto a plate.
5. Transfer the butter into the bowl with the spices. Repeat with the remaining butter and sage leaves. Put some aside for decoration.
6. Put the fried sage leaves onto the mortar and squash them with the pestle. Add the squashed sage to the butter along with the oregano, lemon juice, and tequila and season with salt. Keep warm.
7. Set up the grill. Line a platter with rock salt. Grill the oysters over high heat until they open, about 1 to 2 minutes.
8. Dispose of the top shell and spot the oysters on the rock salt, being careful not to spill their juice.
9. Spoon the warm tequila sauce over the oysters, decorate with a fresh sage leaf, and serve.

SHOPPING LIST

- 1/2 tsp fennel seeds
- 1/4 tsp crushed red pepper
- 7 tbsp of unsalted butter
- 1/4 cup of sage leaves, plus 36 small leaves for the garnish
- 1 tsp of dried oregano
- 2 tbsp lemon juice
- 2 tbsp of tequila
- Kosher salt
- rock salt, for the serving
- 3 dozen scrubbed medium oysters

20 MINUTES

5 MINUTES

6

Citrus Soy Squid

 NUTRITION

Calories: 110, Fat: 6g,
Carbs: 6g, Protein: 8g

 INTOLERANCES

Gluten-Free
Egg-Free
Lactose-Free

15 MINUTES

 **SHOPPING LIST**

- 1 cup mirin
- 1 cup of soy sauce
- 1/3 cup yuzu juice or fresh lemon juice
- 2 cups of water
- 2 pounds squid tentacles left whole; bodies cut crosswise 1 inch thick

 DIRECTIONS

1. In a bowl, mix the mirin, soy sauce, the yuzu juice, and water.
2. Put a bit of the marinade in a container and refrigerate it for later use.
3. Add the squid to the bowl with the rest of the marinade and let it sit for about 30 minutes or refrigerate for 4 hours.
4. Set up the grill. Drain the squid.
5. Grill over medium-high heat, turning once until white all through for 3 minutes.
6. Serve hot.

5 MINUTES

4

Spiced Salmon Kebabs

NUTRITION

Calories: 230, Fat: 10g,
Carbs: 1g, Protein: 30g

INTOLERANCES:

Gluten-Free
Egg-Free
Lactose-Free

4

20
MINUTES

SHOPPING LIST

- 2 tbsp of chopped fresh oregano
- 2 tsp of sesame seeds
- 1 tsp ground cumin
- 1 tsp Kosher salt

- 1/4 tsp crushed red pepper flakes
- 1 1/2 pounds of skinless salmon fillets, cut into 1" pieces

- 2 lemons, thinly sliced into rounds
- 2 tbsp of olive oil
- 16 bamboo skewers soaked in water for one hour

DIRECTIONS

1. Set up the grill for medium heat. Mix the oregano, sesame seeds, cumin, salt, and red pepper flakes in a little bowl. Put the spice blend aside.
2. String the salmon and the lemon slices onto 8 sets of parallel skewers in order to make 8 kebabs.
3. Spoon with oil and season with the spice blend.
4. Grill and turn at times until the fish is cooked.

15
MINUTES

Cod with butter and grilled onions

 **NUTRITION**

Calories: 140, Fat: 5g,
Cholesterol: 46mg,
Carbs: 4g, Protein: 20g

 INTOLERANCES:

Gluten-Free
Egg-Free

 10 MINUTES

 10 MINUTES

 SHOPPING LIST

- 1/4 cup butter
- 1 finely chopped small onion
- 1/4 cup white wine
- 4 (6ounce) cod fillets
- 1 tbsp of extra virgin olive oil
- 1/2 tsp salt (or to taste)
- 1/2 tsp black pepper
- Lemon wedges

DIRECTIONS

 4

1. Set up the grill for medium-high heat.
2. In a little skillet liquefy the butter. Add the onion and cook for 1or 2 minutes.
3. Add the white wine and let stew for an extra 3 minutes. Take away and let it cool for 5 minutes.
4. Spoon the fillets with extra virgin olive oil and sprinkle with salt and pepper. Put the fish on a well-oiled rack and cook for 8 minutes.
5. Season it with sauce and cautiously flip it over. Cook for 6 to 7 minutes more, turning more times or until the fish arrives at an inside temperature of 145°F.
6. Take away from the grill, top with lemon wedges, and serve.

Grilled Calamari with Mustard Oregano and Parsley Sauce

5 MINUTES

8

10 MINUTES

SHOPPING LIST

- 8 Calamari, cleaned
- 2 cups of milk
- Sauce
- 4 tsp of sweet

- mustard
- Juice from 2 lemons
- 1/2 cup of olive oil
- 2 tbsp fresh oregano,

- finely chopped
- Pepper, ground
- 1/2 bunch of parsley, finely chopped

DIRECTIONS

1. Clean calamari well and cut into slices.
2. Place calamari in a large metal bow, cover and marinate with milk overnight.
3. Remove calamari from the milk and drain well on paper towel. Grease the fish lightly with olive oil.
4. In a bowl, combine mustard and the juice from the two lemons.
5. Beat lightly and pour the olive oil very slowly; stir until all the ingredients are combined well.
6. Add the oregano and pepper and stir well.
7. Start the pellet grill and set the temperature to moderate; preheat, lid closed, for 10 to 15 minutes.
8. Place the calamari on the grill and cook for 2-3 minutes per side or until it has a bit of char and remove from the grill.
9. Transfer calamari to serving platter and pour them over with mustard sauce and chopped parsley.

Grilled Cuttlefish with Spinach and Pine Nuts Salad

 NUTRITION

Calories: 299, Fat: 19g,
Cholesterol: 186mg,
Carbs: 3g, Protein: 28g

INTOLERANCES:

Gluten-Free
Egg-Free
Lactose-Free

5 MINUTES

8

15 MINUTES

 SHOPPING LIST

- 1/2 cup of olive oil
- 1 tbsp of lemon juice
- 1 tsp oregano

- Pinch of salt
- 8 large cuttlefish, cleaned

- Spinach, pine nuts, olive oil and vinegar for serving

DIRECTIONS

1. Prepare marinade with olive oil, lemon juice, oregano and a pinch of salt pepper (be careful, cuttlefish do not need too much salt).
2. Place the cuttlefish in the marinade, tossing to cover evenly. Cover and marinate for about 1 hour.
3. Remove the cuttlefish from marinade and pat dry them on paper towel.
4. Start the pellet grill, and set the temperature to high and preheat, lid closed, for 10 to 15 minutes.
5. Grill the cuttlefish just 3 - 4 minutes on each side.
6. Serve hot with spinach, pine nuts, olive oil, and vinegar.

Dijon Lemon Catfish Fillets on the grill

NUTRITION

Calories: 295, Fat: 24g,
Cholesterol: 58mg, Carbs: 3g
Protein: 16g

INTOLERANCES:

Gluten-Free
Egg-Free
Lactose-Free

15 MINUTES

5 MINUTES

4

SHOPPING LIST

- 1/2 cup olive oil
- Juice of 4 lemons
- 2 tbsp Dijon mustard
- 1/2 tsp salt
- 1 tsp paprika
- Fresh rosemary chopped
- 4 (6- to 8-oz.) catfish fillets, 1/2-inch thick

DIRECTIONS

1. Set the temperature to Medium and preheat, lid closed, for 10 to 15 minutes.
2. Whisk the olive oil, lemon juice, mustard, salt, paprika and chopped rosemary in a bowl.
3. Brush one side of each fish fillet with half of the olive oil-lemon mixture; season with salt and pepper to taste.
4. Grill fillets, covered, 4 to 5 minutes. Turn fillets and brush with remaining olive oil-lemon mixture.
5. Grill 4 to 5 minutes more (do not cover).
6. Remove fish fillets to a serving platter, sprinkle with rosemary and serve.

Grilled Halibut Fillets in Chili Rosemary Marinade

NUTRITION

Calories: 259, Fat: 4g,
Cholesterol: 133mg,
Carbs: 5g, Protein: 51g

INTOLERANCES:

Gluten-Free
Egg-Free
Lactose-Free

SHOPPING LIST

- 1 cup of virgin olive oil
- 2 large red chili peppers, chopped
- 2 cloves garlic, cut into quarters
- 1 bay leaf
- 1 twig of rosemary
- 2 lemons
- 4 tbsp of white vinegar
- 4 halibut fillets

DIRECTIONS

1. In a large container, mix olive oil, chopped red chili, garlic, bay leaf, rosemary, lemon juice and white vinegar.
2. Submerge halibut fillets and toss to combine well.
3. Cover and marinate in the refrigerator for several hours or overnight.
4. Remove anchovies from marinade and pat dry on paper towels for 30 minutes.
5. Start the pellet grill, set the temperature to medium and preheat, lid closed for 10 to 15 minutes.
6. Grill the anchovies, skin side down for about 10 minutes, or until the flesh of the fish becomes white (thinner cuts and fillets can cook in as little time as 6 minutes).
7. Turn once during cooking to avoid having the halibut fall apart.
8. Transfer to a large serving platter, pour a little lemon juice over the fish, sprinkle with rosemary and serve.

Grilled Lobster with Lemon Butter and Parsley

NUTRITION

Calories: 385, Fat: 24g,
Cholesterol: 346mg,
Carbs: 2g, Protein: 37g

INTOLERANCES:

Gluten-Free
Egg-Free

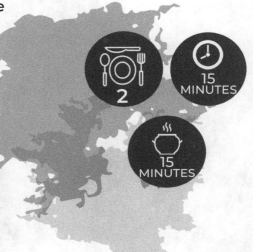

SHOPPING LIST

- 1 lobster (or more)
- 1/2 cup fresh butter
- 2 lemons juice (freshly squeezed)
- 2 tbsp parsley
- Salt and freshly ground pepper to taste

DIRECTIONS

1. Use a pot large enough to hold the lobster(s) and fill water and salt. Bring to boil and put in lobster. Boil for 4 - 5 minutes.
2. Put the lobster on a working surface.
3. Flatten the body to the base of the head and divide the head.
4. Firmly hold the body, with the abdomen upward, and with a sharp knife cut it along in the middle.
5. Start your pellet grill with the lid open until the fire is established (4 to 5 minutes). Set the temperature to 350°F and preheat, lid closed for 10 to 15 minutes.
6. Melt the butter and whisk it with the lemon juice, parsley, salt, and pepper. Spread this butter mixture over the lobster and put directly on the grill grate.
7. Grill the lobsters cut side down about 7 - 8 minutes until the shells are bright in color (also, depends on its size).
8. Turn the lobster over and brush with the butter mixture. Grill for another 4 - 5 minutes.
9. Serve hot sprinkled with lemon butter and finely chopped parsley.

Grilled Trout in White Wine and Parsley Marinade

NUTRITION

Calories: 267, Fat: 18g,
Carbs: 3g, Protein: 16g

INTOLERANCES:

Gluten-Free
Egg-Free
Lactose-Free

SHOPPING LIST

- 1/4 cup olive oil
- 1 lemon juice
- 1/2 cup of white wine
- 2 cloves garlic minced
- 2 tbsp fresh parsley,

finely chopped
- 1 tsp fresh basil, finely chopped
- Salt and freshly ground black pepper

to taste
- 4 trout fish, cleaned
- Lemon slices for garnish

DIRECTIONS

1. In a large container, stir the olive oil, lemon juice, wine, garlic, parsley, basil and salt and freshly ground black pepper to taste.
2. Submerge fish in the sauce and stir to combine well.
3. Cover and marinate in refrigerate overnight.
4. When ready to cook, start the pellet grill on Smoke with the lid open for 4 to 5 minutes. Set the temperature to 400°F and preheat, lid closed, for 10 to 15 minutes.
5. Remove the fish from marinade and pat dry on paper towel; reserve marinade.
6. Grill trout for 5 minutes from both sides (be careful not to overcook the fish).
7. Pour fish with marinade and serve hot with lemon slices.

Stuffed Squid on the Grill

NUTRITION

Calories: 290, Fat: 13g,
Cholesterol: 288mg,
Carbs: 13g, Protein: 25g

INTOLERANCES:

Egg-Free

SHOPPING LIST

- 2 lbs. of squid
- 4 cloves garlic
- 10 sprigs parsley
- 4 slices old bread
- 1/3 cup of milk
- Salt and ground white pepper
- 4 slices of prosciutto
- 4 slices of cheese
- 3 tbsp of olive oil
- 1 lemon

DIRECTIONS

1. Wash and clean your squid and pat dry on paper towel. Finely chop parsley and garlic.
2. Cut bread into cubes and soak in milk.
3. Add parsley, garlic, white pepper and salt. Stir well together.
4. Cut the cheese into larger pieces (the pieces should be large enough that they can be pushed through the opening of the squid).
5. Mix the cheese with prosciutto slices and stir well together with remaining ingredients.
6. Use your fingers to open the bag pack of squid and push the mixture inside. At the end add some more bread.
7. Close the openings with toothpicks.
8. Start your pellet grill on smoke with the lid open for 5 minutes.
9. Set the temperature to the highest setting and preheat, lid closed, for 10 – 15 minutes.
10. Grill squid for 3 – 4 minutes being careful not to burn the squid. Serve hot.

CHAPTER 9

Vegetable Recepies

Smoked Mushrooms

NUTRITION

Calories: 1680, Fat: 30g,
Carbs: 10g, Protein: 4g

INTOLERANCES:

Gluten-Free
Egg-Free
Lactose-Free

SHOPPING LIST

- 4 cup Portobello, whole and cleaned
- 1 tbsp. canola oil
- 1 tbsp. onion powder
- 1 tbsp. granulated garlic
- 1 tbsp. salt
- 1 tbsp. pepper

15
MINUTES

DIRECTIONS

1. Put all the ingredients and mix well.
2. Set the wood pellet temperature to 180°F then place the mushrooms directly on the grill.
3. Smoke the mushrooms for 30 minutes.
4. Increase the temperature to high and cook the mushrooms for a further 15 minutes.
5. Serve and enjoy.

45
MINUTES

Whole Roasted Cauliflower with Garlic Parmesan Butter

 NUTRITION

Calories: 156, Fat: 11.1g,
Carbs: 8.8g, Protein: 8.2g

 **INTOLERANCES:**

Gluten-Free
Egg-Free

 5

 15 MINUTES

 45 MINUTES

 SHOPPING LIST

- 1/4 cup olive oil
- Salt and pepper to taste
- 1 cauliflower, fresh
- 1/2 cup butter, melted
- 1/4 cup parmesan cheese, grated
- 2 garlic cloves, minced
- 1/2 tbsp. parsley, chopped

DIRECTIONS

1. Preheat the wood pellet grill with the lid closed for 15 minutes.
2. Brush the cauliflower with oil then season with salt and pepper.
3. Place the cauliflower in a cast Iron and place it on a grill grate.
4. Cook for 45 minutes or until the cauliflower is golden brown and tender
5. Mix butter, cheese, garlic, and parsley in a mixing bowl.
6. In the last 20 minutes of cooking, add the butter mixture.
7. Remove the cauliflower and top with more cheese and parsley if you desire.
8. Enjoy.

Grilled Asparagus and Honey Glazed Carrots

NUTRITION

Calories: 1680, Fat: 30g,

Carbs: 10g, Protein: 4g

INTOLERANCES:

Gluten-Free

Egg-Free

Lactose-Free

15 MINUTES

35 MINUTES

5

SHOPPING LIST

- 1 bunch asparagus, trimmed ends
- 1 lb. carrots, peeled
- 2 tbsp. olive oil
- Sea salt to taste
- 2 tbsp. honey
- Lemon zest

DIRECTIONS

1. Sprinkle the asparagus with oil and sea salt. Drizzle the carrots with honey and salt.
2. Preheat the wood pellet to 165°F with the lid closed for 15 minutes.
3. Place the carrots in the wood pellet and cook for 15 minutes. Add asparagus and cook for 20 more minutes or until cooked.
4. Top the carrots and asparagus with lemon zest.
5. Enjoy!

Mixed Grilled Vegetables

NUTRITION

Calories: 44, Fat: 5g, Carbs: 1g, Potassium: 10mg

INTOLERANCES:

Gluten-Free
Egg-Free
Lactose-Free

SHOPPING LIST

- 1 veggies (any mixed)
- 1/4 cup vegetable oil
- 2 tbsp. veggie seasoning

8

5 MINUTES

15 MINUTES

DIRECTIONS

1. Preheat the wood pellet grill to 375°F
2. Toss the vegetables in oil then place on a sheet pan.
3. Sprinkle with veggie seasoning then place on the hot grill.
4. Grill for 15 minutes or until the veggies are cooked.
5. Let rest then serve.
6. Enjoy.

Smoked Acorn Squash

NUTRITION

Calories: 149, Fat: 10g,
Carbs: 14g, Protein: 2g

INTOLERANCES:

Gluten-Free
Egg-Free

10 MINUTES

6

SHOPPING LIST

- 3 tbsp. olive oil
- 3 acorn squash, halved and seeded
- 1/4 cup unsalted butter
- 1/4 cup brown sugar
- 1 tbsp. cinnamon, ground
- 1 tbsp. chili powder
- 1 tbsp. nutmeg, ground

DIRECTIONS

1. Cut the squash and brush olive oil on each side. Cover the halves with foil. Poke holes on the foil to allow steam and smoke through.
2. Fire up the wood pellet to 225°F and smoke the squash for 1 ½-2 hour.
3. Remove the squash from the smoker and allow it to sit.
4. Melt butter, sugar and spices in a saucepan. Stir well to combine.
5. Take the squach halves and spread the butter mixture in each squash half.
6. Enjoy.

2 HOURS

Vegan Smoked Carrot Hot dogs

 NUTRITION

Calories: 149, Fat: 1.6g,
Carbs: 27.9g, Protein: 5.4g

 INTOLERANCES

Gluten-Free
Egg-Free
Lactose-Free

 **SHOPPING LIST**

- 4 thick carrots
- 2 tbsp. avocado oil
- 1 tbsp. liquid smoke
- 1/2 tbsp. garlic powder
- Salt and pepper to taste

 DIRECTIONS

1. Preheat the wood pellet grill to 425°F and line a baking sheet with parchment paper.
2. Peel the carrots and round the edges.
3. In a mixing bowl, mix oil, liquid smoke, garlic, salt, and pepper. Place the carrots on the baking dish then pour the mixture over.
4. Roll the carrots to coat evenly with the mixture and use fingertips to massage the mixture into the carrots.
5. Place in the grill and grill for 35 minutes or until the carrots are fork-tender, ensuring to turn and brush the carrots every 5 minutes with the marinade.
6. Remove from the grill and place the carrots in hot dog bun. Serve with your favorite toppings and enjoy.

25 MINUTES

35 MINUTES

4

Grilled Spicy Sweet Potatoes

Calories: 145, Fat: 5g,
Carbs: 23g, Protein: 2g

 INTOLERANCES

Gluten-Free

Egg-Free

Lactose-Free

 **SHOPPING LIST**

- 2 lb. sweet potatoes, cut into chunks
- 1 red onion, chopped
- 2 tbsp. oil
- 2 tbsp. orange juice
- 1 tbsp. roasted cinnamon
- 1 tbsp. salt
- 1/4 tbsp. Chipotle chili pepper

 DIRECTIONS

1. Preheat the wood pellet grill to 425°F with the lid closed.
2. Mix the sweet potatoes with onion, oil, and juice.
3. In a mixing bowl, mix cinnamon, salt, and pepper then sprinkle the mixture over the sweet potatoes.
4. Spread the potatoes on a lined baking dish in a single layer.
5. Place the baking dish in the grill and grill for 30 minutes or until the sweet potatoes are tender.
6. Serve and enjoy.

10 MINUTES · 35 MINUTES · 6

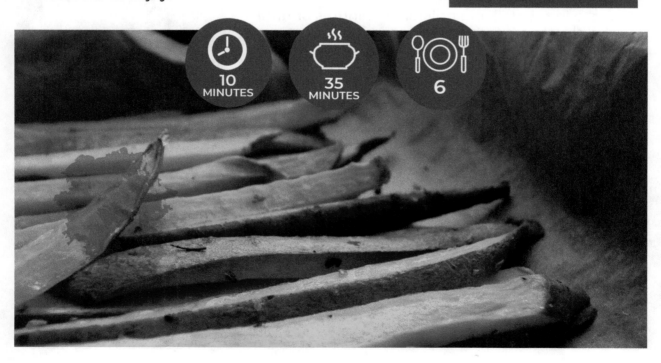

Grilled Mexican Corn (Elote)

 NUTRITION

Calories: 144, Fat: 5g,
Carbs: 10g

 INTOLERANCES

Gluten-Free
Egg-Free

 DIRECTIONS

1. Brush the corn with oil.
2. Sprinkle with salt.
3. Place the corn on a wood pellet grill set at 350°F. Cook for 25 minutes as you turn it occasionally.
4. Mix mayo, cream, garlic, chili, and red pepper until well combined.
5. Let it rest for some minutes then brush with the mayo mixture.
6. Sprinkle cottage cheese, more chili powder, and cilantro.
7. Serve with lime wedges. Enjoy.

 SHOPPING LIST

- 6 ears of corn on the cob
- 1 tbsp. olive oil
- Kosher salt and pepper to taste
- 1/4 cup mayo
- 1/4 cup sour cream
- 1 tbsp. garlic paste
- 1/2 tbsp. chili powder
- Pinch of ground red pepper
- 1/2 cup coria cheese, crumbled
- 1/4 cup cilantro, chopped
- 6 lime wedges

5 MINUTES

25 MINUTES

6

Smoked Asparagus

NUTRITION

Calories: 43,Fat: 2g,

Carbs: 4g,Protein: 3g

INTOLERANCES

Gluten-Free

Egg-Free

Lactose-Free

SHOPPING LIST

- 1 bunch fresh asparagus ends cut
- 2 tbsp. olive oil
- Salt and pepper to taste

DIRECTIONS

1. Fire up your wood pellet smoker to 230°F
2. Place the asparagus in a mixing bowl and drizzle with olive oil. Season with salt and pepper.
3. Place the asparagus in a tinfoil sheet and fold the sides such that you create a basket.
4. Smoke the asparagus for 1 hour or until soft turning after half an hour.
5. Remove from the grill and serve.
6. Enjoy.

5 MINUTES | 1 HOUR | 4

Perfectly Smoked Artichoke Hearts

NUTRITION

Calories: 105, Fat: 1g
Carbs: 19g, Protein: 7g

INTOLERANCES

Gluten-Free
Egg-Free
Lactose-Free

SHOPPING LIST

- 12 canned whole artichoke hearts
- 1/4 cup of extra virgin olive oil
- 4 cloves of garlic minced
- 2 Tbsp of fresh parsley finely chopped (leaves)
- 1 Tbsp of fresh lemon juice freshly squeezed
- Salt to taste
- Lemon for garnish

DIRECTIONS

1. Start the pellet grill on smoke with the lid open until the fire is established. Set the temperature to 350° and preheat, lid closed, for 10 to 15 minutes.
2. In a bowl, combine all remaining ingredients and pour over artichokes.
3. Place artichokes on a grill rack and smoke for 2 hours or so.
4. Serve hot with extra olive oil, and lemon halves.

10 MINUTES

2 HOUR

6

Finely Smoked Russet Potatoes

NUTRITION

Calories: 380, Fat: 18g
Carbs: 48g, Protein: 6g

INTOLERANCES

Gluten-Free
Egg-Free
Lactose-Free

SHOPPING LIST

- 8 large Russet potatoes
- 1/2 cup of garlic-infused olive oil
- Kosher salt and black pepper to taste

DIRECTIONS

1. Start the pellet grill on "smoke" with the lid open until the fire is established.
2. Set the temperature to 225° and preheat, lid closed, for 10 to 15 minutes.
3. Rinse and dry your potatoes; pierce with a fork on all sides.
4. Drizzle with garlic-infused olive oil and rub generously all your potatoes with the salt and pepper.
5. Place the potatoes on the pellet smoker and close the lid.
6. Smoke potatoes for about 2 hours.
7. Serve hot with your favorite dressing.

6

15
MINUTES

2
HOUR

Simple Smoked Green Cabbage

 NUTRITION

Calories: 50, Fat: 0.2g
Carbs: 10g, Protein: 3g

 INTOLERANCES

Gluten-Free
Egg-Free
Lactose-Free

 SHOPPING LIST

- 1 medium head of green cabbage
- 1/2 cup of olive oil
- Salt and ground white pepper to taste

 DIRECTIONS

1. Start the pellet grill on smoke with the lid open until the fire is established. Set the temperature to 250° and preheat, lid closed, for 10 to 15 minutes.
2. Clean and rinse cabbage under running water.
3. Cut the stem and then cut it in half, then each half in 2 to 3 pieces.
4. Season generously cabbage with the salt and white ground pepper; drizzle with olive oil.
5. Arrange the cabbage peace on their side on a smoker tray and cover.
6. Smoke the cabbage for 20 minutes per side.
7. Remove cabbage and let rest for 5 minutes.
8. Serve immediately.

 4

 5 MINUTES

 45 MINUTES

Cob with Spicy Rub

 NUTRITION

Calories: 240, Fat: 15g

Carbs: 25g, Protein: 4g

 INTOLERANCES

Gluten-Free

Egg-Free

Lactose-Free

SHOPPING LIST

- 10 ears of fresh sweet corn on the cob
- 1/2 cup of macadamia nut oil
- Kosher salt and fresh ground black pepper to taste
- 1/2 tsp of garlic powder
- 1/2 tsp of hot paprika flakes
- 1/2 tsp of dried parsley
- 1/4 tsp of ground mustard

 DIRECTIONS

1. Start the pellet grill on smoke with the lid open until the fire is established. Set the temperature to 350° and preheat, lid closed, for 10 to 15 minutes.
2. Combine macadamia nut oil with garlic powder, hot paprika flakes, dried parsley, and ground mustard.
3. Rub your corn with macadamia nut oil mixture and place on a grill rack.
4. Smoke corn for 80 to 90 minutes.
5. Serve hot.

4

10 MINUTES

1HR 30 MINUTES

Fall Pumpkin Pie

 NUTRITION

Calories: 16, Fat: 14g

Carbs: 10g, Protein: 1g

 INTOLERANCES

Gluten-Free

Egg-Free

Lactose-Free

 SHOPPING LIST

- 4 small pumpkins
- Avocado oil to taste

 DIRECTIONS

1. Start the pellet grill on smoke with the lid open until the fire is established. Set the temperature to 250° and preheat, lid closed, for 10 to 15 minutes.
2. Cut pumpkins in half, top to bottom, and drizzle with avocado oil.
3. Place pumpkin halves on the smoker away from the fire.
4. Smoke pumpkins from 1 1/2 to 2 hours.
5. Remove pumpkins from smoked and allow to cool.
6. Serve

 15 MINUTES

 2 HOURS

 6

Veggies "Potpourri"

 NUTRITION

Calories: 330, Fat: 21g
Carbs: 25g, Protein: 4g

 INTOLERANCES

Gluten-Free
Egg-Free
Lactose-Free

 **SHOPPING LIST**

- 2 large zucchinis sliced
- 2 red bell peppers sliced
- Russet potatoes sliced
- 1 red onion sliced
- 1/2 cup of olive oil
- Salt and ground black pepper to taste

 DIRECTIONS

1. Start the pellet grill on smoke with the lid open until the fire is established. Set the temperature to 350° and preheat, lid closed, for 10 to 15 minutes.
2. Rinse and slice all vegetables; pat dry on a kitchen paper.
3. Generously season with the salt and pepper, and drizzle with olive oil.
4. Place your sliced vegetables into grill basket or onto grill rack and smoke for 40 to 45 minutes.
5. Serve hot.

10 MINUTES

1 HOUR

6

CHAPTER 10

Smoked Recipes

Smoked Chicken Wings

 NUTRITION

Calories: 520, Fat: 40g

Carbs: 5g, Protein: 30g

 INTOLERANCES

Gluten-Free

Egg-Free

Lactose-Free

 DIRECTIONS

1. Pour the olive oil into a pan over medium heat.
2. Cook the onion and garlic for 5 minutes.
3. Add the rest of the sauce ingredients.
4. Cook for 3 minutes, stirring. Increase heat and bring to a boil.
5. Reduce heat and simmer for 20 minutes.
6. Strain out the garlic and onion and transfer to a glass jar with lid. Refrigerate until ready to use.
7. Toss the chicken wings in the vegetable oil. Coat with the dry rub.
8. Load the wood pellets to the hopper. Turn on the smoker.
9. Set the pellet grill to smoke setting. Heat on the smoke while the lid is still open for 5 minutes.
10. Add the chicken wings to the grill.
11. Set it to 250°F. Close the lid.
12. Smoke for 2 hours.
13. Take the sauce out of the refrigerator.
14. Baste the chicken with the sauce.
15. Cook the chicken in the grill for 3 minutes per side.
16. Let rest for 5 minutes before serving.

 **SHOPPING LIST**

Sauce:
- 1 teaspoon olive oil
- 1/2 onion, minced
- 5 cloves garlic, minced
- 2 cups ketchup
- 1/4 cup tomato paste
- 1/4 cup Worcestershire sauce
- 1/4 cup apple cider vinegar
- 2 tablespoon liquid smoke
- 1/2 cup packed light brown sugar
- 1 teaspoon hot sauce
- 1/4 teaspoon cayenne pepper
- Salt and pepper to taste

Chicken Wings:
- 4 lb. chicken wings
- Sweet dry rub
- 2 tablespoons vegetable oil

Smoked Brisket

INTOLERANCES

Gluten-Free
Egg-Free
Lactose-Free

20 MINUTES

6 HR 30 MINUTES

10

SHOPPING LIST

Sauce:
- 1/3 cup olive oil
- 1 cup red wine vinegar
- 1 cup white vinegar
- 1/2 cup Worcestershire sauce
- 1 tablespoon brown sugar
- 1 teaspoon garlic powder
- 1 teaspoon cumin
- 1 teaspoon paprika
- 1/2 teaspoon cayenne pepper
- 1 teaspoon honey
- Salt and pepper to taste

Brisket:
- 5 lb. brisket
- Any dry rub

DIRECTIONS

1. Put all the sauce ingredients in a pot.
2. Bring to a boil.
3. Reduce heat and simmer for 8 to 10 minutes. Transfer to a bowl.
4. Set the wood pellet grill to smoke setting to 150°F.
5. Coat the brisket with the dry rub. Place it on the grill.
6. Close the grill and smoke for 2 hours. Transfer the brisket to a baking pan.
7. Increase the setting to 250°.
8. Brush the brisket with the sauce.
9. Smoke for 4 hours, brushing the brisket with the sauce every 30 minutes.

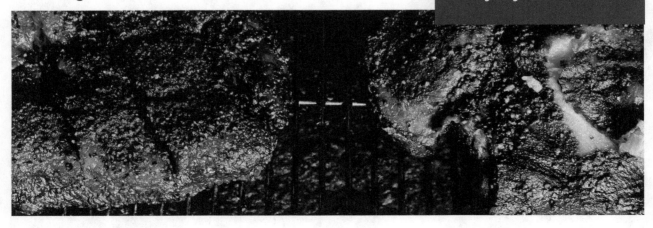

Smoked Beef Ribs

 **NUTRITION**

Calories: 340, Fat: 25g
Cholesterol: 95mg, Protein: 25g

 **INTOLERANCES:**

Gluten-Free
Egg-Free
Lactose-Free

25 MINUTES

8 HOURS

 SHOPPING LIST

- 4 lb. beef ribs
- 1 tablespoon spicy brown mustard
- 2 tablespoons beef and brisket rub
- 1/3 cup beef stock
- 1 onion, sliced into wedges
- 4 cloves garlic, crushed
- 2 lb. tomato, cubed
- 1 tablespoon olive oil
- Salt and pepper to taste
- 1/2 cup water
- 1 1/3 cup apple cider vinegar
- 2 teaspoons paprika
- 1/4 teaspoon cayenne pepper
- 1/4 cup molasses
- 2 tablespoons honey

DIRECTIONS

1. Set the wood pellet grill to smoke. Rub the ribs with the mustard.
2. Sprinkle with the dry rub. Use a syrenge to inject the stock into the meat.
3. Set the temperature to 250°F.
4. Smoke the ribs for 3 hours.
5. Add the onion, garlic and tomato in a baking pan.
6. Pour olive oil on top and sprinkle with the salt and pepper.
7. Add the tray to the smoker.
8. Pour the water and vinegar into a grill pan.
9. Place beside the ribs. Increase heat to 275°F.
10. Smoke for 4 hours.
11. Transfer the smoked tomatoes to a blender.
12. Add the rest of the ingredients. Blend until smooth.
13. Brush the ribs with the sauce.
14. Serve the remaining sauce with the cooked ribs.

Smoked Pork Belly

NUTRITION

Calories: 300
Fat: 25g
Protein: 17g

INTOLERANCES:

Gluten-Free
Egg-Free
Lactose-Free

20 MINUTES

6 HR 30 MINUTES

15

SHOPPING LIST

- Peanut oil
- Habanero dry rub
- 13 lb. pork belly
- Salt to taste
- 1 cup sweet barbecue sauce

DIRECTIONS

1. Add the pork belly to a cutting board. Score the fat and skin.
2. Season with the salt and dry rub. Marinate for 15 minutes.
3. Set the wood pellet grill to smoke to 250°F.
4. Add the pork belly to the grill.
5. Smoke for 6 hours.
6. Brush the barbecue sauce on the sides of the belly. Cook for 5 minutes.
7. Wrap the pork belly in foil. Grill for 15 minutes.

Smoked Duck Breast

NUTRITION

Calories: 270, Fat: 20g
Carbs: 1g, Protein: 17g

INTOLERANCES:

Gluten-Free
Egg-Free
Lactose-Free

15 MINUTES

2 HOURS

4

SHOPPING LIST

- 2 lb. duck breast
- 2 tablespoons maple syrup
- 2 tablespoons smoky dry rub

DIRECTIONS

1. Add the duck breast to a baking pan.
2. In a bowl, mix the maple syrup and dry rub.
3. Coat the duck breast with the mixture. Cover with foil.
4. Refrigerate overnight.
5. Set the wood pellet grill to smoke to 375°F. Smoke it for 2 hours.
6. Score the duck with shallow cuts.
7. Increase temperature to 500°F.
8. Sear both sides of the duck for 5 minutes.
9. Serve.

Smoked Pepper Baby Back Ribs

20 MINUTES

5 HOURS

4

NUTRITION

Calories: 660, Fat: 42g
Cholesterol: 130mg,Carbs: 48g
Protein: 28g

INTOLERANCES:

Gluten-Free

Egg-Free

SHOPPING LIST

- 2 racks baby back ribs
- 1/4 cup yellow mustard
- 1/4 cup sweet dry rub
- 1/2 cup dark brown sugar
- 1 cup melted butter
- 12 oz. soda, divided
- 1 cup barbecue sauce

DIRECTIONS

1. Add the ribs to a baking tray.
2. Coat the ribs with the mustard.
3. Sprinkle with the dry rub.
4. Set the wood pellet grill to smoke. Preheat it to 225°F.
5. Add the ribs to the grill. Smoke the ribs for 2 hours.
6. In a bowl, mix the brown sugar, butter and 8 oz. soda. Add half of this mixture to a baking pan.
7. Add the ribs to the baking pan.
8. Pour the remaining mixture on top of the ribs. Cover with foil.
9. Smoke for another 2 hours. Take it out of the pan.
10. Cook for another 1 hour or until ribs are tender.

Smoked Avocado Pork Ribs

NUTRITION

Calories: 675, Fat: 64g

Carbs: 0.9g, Protein: 28g

INTOLERANCES:

Gluten-Free

Egg-Free

Lactose-Free

20 MINUTES

3 HR 20 MINUTES

5

SHOPPING LIST

- 2 lbs. of pork spareribs
- 1 cup of avocado oil
- 1 tsp of garlic powder
- 1 tsp of onion powder
- 1 tsp of sweet pepper flakes
- Salt and pepper, to taste

DIRECTIONS

1. In a bowl, combine the avocado oil, garlic salt, garlic powder, onion powder, sweet pepper flakes, and salt and pepper.
2. Place pork chops in a shallow container and pour evenly avocado mixture.
3. Cover and refrigerate for at least 4 hours, or overnight.
4. Start pellet grill on, lid open, until the fire is established (4-5 minutes). Increase the temperature to 225° and allow to pre-heat, lid closed, for 10 - 15 minutes.
5. Arrange pork chops on the grill rack and smoke for about 3 to 4 hours.
6. Transfer pork chops on serving plate, let them rest for 15 minutes and serve.

Smoked Honey & Garlic Pork Chops

📖 NUTRITION

Calories: 301, Carbs: 17g
Fat: 6g, Protein: 41g

📖 INTOLERANCES:

Gluten-Free
Egg-Free
Lactose-Free

20 MINUTES

1 HR 15 MINUTES

4

🧺 SHOPPING LIST

- 1/4 cup of lemon juice freshly squeezed
- 1/4 cup honey (preferably a darker honey)
- 3 cloves garlic, minced
- 2 tbsp. soy sauce (or tamari sauce)
- Salt and pepper to taste
- 24 ounces center-cut pork chops boneless

DIRECTIONS

1. Combine honey, lemon juice, soy sauce, garlic and the salt and pepper in a bowl.
2. Place pork in a container and pour marinade over pork.
3. Cover and marinate in a fridge overnight.
4. Remove pork from marinade and pat dry on kitchen paper towel. (reserve marinade)
5. Start your pellet on Smoke with the lid open until the fire is established (4 - 5 minutes). Increase temperature to 450° and preheat, lid closed, for 10 - 15 minutes.
6. Arrange the pork chops on the grill racks and smoke for about one hour (depending on the thickness).
7. In a meantime, heat remaining marinade in a small saucepan over medium heat to simmer.
8. Transfer pork chops on a serving plate, pour with the marinade and serve hot.

Smoked Pork Burgers

NUTRITION

Calories: 580, Carbs: 1g
Fat: 48g, Protein: 38.4g

INTOLERANCES:

Gluten-Free
Egg-Free
Lactose-Free

20 MINUTES

1 HR 30 MINUTES

4

SHOPPING LIST

- 2 lbs. ground pork
- 1/2 of onion finely chopped
- 2 tbsp. fresh sage, chopped
- 1 tsp. garlic powder
- 1 tsp. cayenne pepper
- Salt and pepper to taste

DIRECTIONS

1. Start the pellet grill (recommended hickory pellet) on smoke with the lid open until the fire is established.
2. Set the temperature to 225° and preheat, lid closed, for 10 to 15 minutes.
3. In a bowl, combine ground pork with all remaining ingredients.
4. Use your hands to mix thoroughly. Form mixture into 8 evenly burgers.
5. Place the hamburgers on the racks.
6. Smoke the burgers for 60 to 90 minutes until they reach an internal temperature of 150 to 160°F.
7. Serve hot.

Smoked Spicy Pork Medallions

NUTRITION

Calories: 360, Carbs: 4g
Fat: 14g, Protein: 52g

INTOLERANCES:

Gluten-Free
Egg-Free
Lactose-Free

6 | 20 MINUTES | 1 HR 45 MINUTES

SHOPPING LIST

- 2 lbs. pork medallions
- 3/4 cup chicken stock
- 1/2 cup tomato sauce (organic)
- 2 tbsp. of smoked hot paprika (or to taste)
- 2 tbsp. of fresh basil finely chopped
- 1 tbsp. oregano
- Salt and pepper to taste

DIRECTIONS

1. In a bowl, combine the chicken stock, tomato sauce, paprika, oregano, salt, and pepper.
2. Brush generously over the outside of the tenderloin.
3. Start the pellet grill on Smoke with the lid open until the fire is established (4 to 5 minutes).
4. Set the temperature to 250F and preheat, lid closed, for 10 to 15 minutes.
5. Place the pork on the grill grate and smoke until the internal temperature of the pork is at least medium-rare (about 145°), for 1 1/2 hours.
6. Let meat rest for 15 minutes and serve.

Smoked Pork Cutlets with Caraway and Dill

📖 NUTRITION

Calories: 300, Carbs: 2g
Fat: 18g, Protein: 32g

📖 INTOLERANCES:

Gluten-Free
Egg-Free
Lactose-Free

1 HR 45 MINUTES

4

20 MINUTES

🧺 SHOPPING LIST

- 4 pork cutlets
- 2 lemons freshly squeezed
- 2 tbsp. fresh parsley

finely chopped
- 1 tbsp. of ground caraway
- 3 tbsp. of fresh dill

finely chopped
- 1/4 cup of olive oil
- Salt and ground black pepper

🛍 DIRECTIONS

1. Place the pork cutlets in a large resealable bag along with all remaining ingredients; shake to combine well.
2. Refrigerate for at least 4 hours.
3. Remove the pork cutlets from marinade and pat dry on kitchen towel.
4. Start the pellet grill (recommended maple pellet) on smoke with the lid open until the fire is established.
5. Set the temperature to 250° and preheat, lid closed, for 10 to 15 minutes.
6. Arrange pork cutlets on the grill rack and smoke for about 1 1/2 hours.
7. Allow cooling on room temperature before serving.

Balsamic–Glazed Baby Back Ribs

SHOPPING LIST

Rub
- 2 tablespoons dark brown sugar
- Salt or to taste
- 2 tablespoons granulated sugar
- 1 tablespoon paprika
- 1/4 teaspoon ground

white pepper
- 1/4 teaspoon ground black pepper
- 1/4 teaspoon ground mustard
- 1/4 teaspoon dried thyme
- 1 teaspoon garlic

powder
- 1 teaspoon ground Szechuan peppercorns
- 1/2 teaspoon cayenne pepper
- 3 racks baby back ribs
- 2 cups balsamic barbecue sauce

DIRECTIONS

1. Take a mixing bowl and combine all the ingredients in it.
2. Preheat the smoker grill at 225°F until the smoke started to appear.
3. Rub the pork ribs with the spices from the bowl and set aside for a few minutes.
4. Once the smoker grill is preheated, place the ribs onto the grill grate.
5. Close the lid and cook the meat for 4 hours at 225°F.
6. After every 1 hour, baste the ribs with BBQ sauce with the help of a brush.
7. Once the cooking time completes, take out the ribs and serve.
8. Let it sit at room temperature before cutting and serving.

4 HOURS

Smoked Trout

NUTRITION

Calories: 110, Fat: 6g
Protein: 14g

INTOLERANCES:

Gluten-Free
Egg-Free
Lactose-Free

2 HOURS

6

15 MINUTES

SHOPPING LIST

- 4 Trout fillets, bones removed

Rub:
- 1/2 teaspoon Onion powder
- 1 ½ teaspoon Salt
- 1/4 teaspoon Ground black pepper
- 1/2 teaspoon Red chili powder
- 2 tablespoons Brown sugar
- 1 teaspoon Dried oregano
- 1/2 teaspoon Dried thyme

DIRECTIONS

1. Fill hopper of the smoker with hardwood pellets, any flavor, and set drip pan over the fire pot.
2. Plug in the smoker and set the temperature to 225°F using the control panel.
3. Wait for 10 to 15 minutes or until the fire starts in the grill and smoker reach to the desired temperature.
4. In the meantime, prepare fish.
5. Stir together all the ingredients for rub and then season well on all sides of trout.
6. When smoker preheats, place seasoned trout on the grill, close with a lid and let smoke for 2 hours or until internal temperature reach to 140°F.
7. While smoking, fill the hopper with more hardwood every half an hour to maintain the temperature in the grill.
8. Serve when ready.

Smoked Lobster Tails

NUTRITION

Calories: 130, Fat: 1g
Protein: 27g

INTOLERANCES:

Gluten-Free
Egg-Free

20 MINUTES

1 HOUR

4

SHOPPING LIST

- 3 Lobster tail
- 1/2 teaspoon Minced garlic
- 1/2 cup Melted butter
- 1/2 teaspoon Salt
- 1/2 teaspoon Ground black pepper

DIRECTIONS

1. Fill hopper of the smoker with hardwood pellets, any flavor, and set drip pan over the fire pot.
2. Plug in the smoker and set the temperature to 400°F using the control panel.
3. Wait for 10 to 15 minutes or until the fire starts in the grill and smoker reach to the desired temperature.
4. In the meantime, prepare lobster tails.
5. Melt butter and then stir in garlic until combined.
6. Split the tail using a sharp knife and brush garlic butter on the exposed meat.
7. When smoker preheats, place lobster tails on the grill, close with a lid and let smoke for 1 hour or until internal temperature reach to 135°F.
8. While smoking, fill the hopper with more hardwood every half an hour to maintain the temperature in the grill.
9. When done, remove lobster from the smoker, transfer meat from tail to a serving plate.
10. Season with salt and black pepper and serve.

Smoked Sea Scallops

 NUTRITION

Calories: 90g, Fat: 5g
Carbs: 1g, Protein: 14g

 **INTOLERANCES**

Gluten-Free
Egg-Free

 DIRECTIONS

1. Fill hopper of the smoker with hardwood pellets, any flavor, and set drip pan over the fire pot.
2. Plug in the smoker and set the temperature to 400°F using the control panel.
3. Wait for 10 to 15 minutes or until the fire starts in the grill and smoker reach to the desired temperature.
4. Before setting smoker, prepare scallops.
5. Rinse scallops under cold water, pat dry and season with salt and black pepper.
6. Arrange scallops in a single layer on a rimmed baking sheet, then place on a heated grill grate.
7. Let smoke for 20 minutes, then increase heat to 400°F and continue smoking for 15 minutes or until tender.
8. Place butter in a small saucepan over medium-low heat and when melted, whisk in garlic, parsley, orange zest, Worcestershire sauce, and orange juice until combined.
9. Simmer for 5 minutes and set aside until required.
10. Serve scallops with the prepared sauce.

SHOPPING LIST

- 2 pounds Scallops
- 1 ½ teaspoon Salt
- 1 teaspoon Ground black pepper

Sauce:
- 1 teaspoon Minced garlic
- 1/2 Small orange, zested
- 1 1/2 teaspoon Chopped parsley
- 8 tablespoons Melted butter
- 1/4 teaspoon Worcestershire sauce
- 1/2 Small orange juice

6 | 15 MINUTES | 35 MINUTES

Smoked Venison Steaks

 NUTRITION

Calories: 130, Fat: 2g
Carbs: 1g, Protein: 25g

 INTOLERANCES

Gluten-Free
Egg-Free
Lactose-Free

 **SHOPPING LIST**

- 1-pound Venison backstrap steaks
- 2 tablespoons Game/BBQ rub

 DIRECTIONS

1. Fill hopper of the smoker with hardwood pellets, any flavor, and set drip pan over the fire pot.
2. Plug in the smoker and set the temperature to 225°F using the control panel.
3. Wait for 10 to 15 minutes or until the fire starts in the grill and smoker reach to the desired temperature.
4. Before preheating smoker, prepare venison.
5. Season venison steaks with rub and let marinate for 20 minutes.
6. When smoker preheats, place steaks on the grill, close with a lid and let smoke for 30 to 45 minutes or until internal temperature reaches to 110°F.
7. Transfer steaks a cutting board and let rest for 10 minutes before serving.

15 MINUTES

35 MINUTES

4

229

Cheesy Smoked Zucchini with Pulled Pork

NUTRITION

Calories: 189, Fat: 10g
Carbs: 11g, Protein: 17g

INTOLERANCES

Gluten-Free
Egg-Free

10

SHOPPING LIST

- 3 lbs. Zucchini
- Topping:
- 2 cups Pulled pork
- 2 cups Grated Mozzarella cheese
- 2 tablespoons Black pepper

DIRECTIONS

1. Preheat the smoker until it reaches the desired temperature prior to smoking.
2. Use apple wood chips for the smoking.
3. Cut the zucchini into halves lengthwise then discard the seeds.
4. Fill each halved zucchini with pulled pork then top with grated Mozzarella cheese.
5. Sprinkle black pepper over the zucchini then set aside.
6. Fill the hopper with soaked apple wood chips then select "smoke" on the wood pellet smoker. Let the lid open.
7. Program the temperature to 375°F (191°C) then close the lid.
8. Arrange the filled zucchini on the rack of a wood pellet smoker then smoke for about 40 minutes or until the cheese is melted.
9. Once it is done, remove from the smoker and arrange on a serving dish.
10. Serve and enjoy immediately.

15 MINUTES

50 MINUTES

Summer Noodle Salad with Cucumber and Smoked Tofu

 NUTRITION

Calories: 330, Fat: 7g

Carbs: 55g, Protein: 10g

 INTOLERANCES

Gluten-Free

Egg-Free

 **SHOPPING LIST**

- 100g glass noodles
- 1 clove of garlic
- 2 tbsp. peanut oil
- 2 tsp. sesame seeds
- 1/2 red bell pepper
- 2 tomatoes
- 1 mini cucumber
- 1 small red chili pepper
- 2 tbsp brown sugar
- 6 tablespoons of lime juice
- 3 tbsp fish sauce
- 2 tbsp peanut oil
- 4 stems of coriander green
- 2 stalks of Thai basil, (alternatively basil)
- 200g smoked tofu
- 2 tbsp peanut oil
- 3 tbsp soy sauce

 DIRECTIONS

1. Pour boiling water over 100g of glass noodles in a bowl, let steep for 5 minutes, pour into a sieve, quench and drain well. Cut the pasta short with the scissors to fit your mouth.
2. Cut 1 clove of garlic into thin slices, fry in a pan in 2 tablespoons of peanut oil, light brown and drain on kitchen paper. Roast 2 tsp sesame seeds in a pan without fat until light brown.
3. Clean and core 1/2 red bell pepper and dice 5 mm. Dice 2 tomatoes and 1 mini cucumber 5mm.
4. Cut 1 small red chili pepper with seeds into fine rings. Mix 2 tablespoons of brown sugar with 5-6 tablespoons of lime juice, 2-3 tablespoons of fish sauce, chili, 2 tablespoons of peanut oil and 3 tablespoons of water.
5. Mix everything with the pasta and let it steep for 5 minutes. Pluck leaves from 4 stalks of coriander green and 2 stalks of Thai basil (alternatively basil) and roughly chop, mix half of them with the salad.
6. Cut 200g of smoked tofu into 5mm slices and fry in a pan in 2 tablespoons of peanut oil on both sides light brown.
7. Deglaze with 2-3 tbsp soy sauce, swirl briefly and serve with the glass noodles. Sprinkle the remaining herbs on top.

15 MINUTES

20 MINUTES

4

Braised Cabbage with Smoked Tofu

 NUTRITION

Calories: 98, Fat: 5g
Carbs: 6g, Protein: 7g

 INTOLERANCES

Gluten-Free
Egg-Free

 **SHOPPING LIST**

- 800g white cabbage
- 2 onions
- 4 tablespoons of oil
- 3 tbsp tomato paste
- salt
- pepper
- 1 tsp marjoram
- dried
- 500ml vegetable broth
- 1 bunch of parsley
- 50g mountain cheese
- 200g tofu

DIRECTIONS

1. Clean the white cabbage, cut out the thick stalk in a wedge shape and cut the leaves into 3 cm pieces. Halve onions and cut into strips.
2. Braise both in a large saucepan in 3 tablespoons of hot oil for 5 minutes over medium heat. Add tomato paste and sauté for 2 minutes.
3. Season well with salt, pepper and marjoram. Pour in the broth, bring to the boil and simmer for 30 minutes over medium to mild heat.
4. Now pluck the parsley leaves and chop them finely. Grate mountain cheese. Pat the tofu dry and dice it small. Fry tofu in a pan with 1 tablespoon of oil all over on a high heat.
5. Mix the tofu cubes into the white cabbage. Sprinkle with mountain cheese and cover and let melt for 5 minutes. Serve sprinkled with parsley.

 15 MINUTES

 **40 MINUTES**

Smoked Salmon Fillet

 NUTRITION

Calories: 115, Fat: 5g
Protein: 19g

 DIRECTIONS

1. Using tweezers, remove any bones that may remain in the salmon fillet. Sponge the fillets with paper towels. The drier the fish, the better.
2. Rub the salmon with the fish spices. Cover and let stand.
3. Prepare your smokehouse. Take a casserole dish in which you can place a cooking basket or a stainless-steel grid and which you can close tightly.
4. Place the sawdust in a small pile on the bottom of the casserole dish with the fennel and a lemon cut into pieces. Place the basket or rack on top.
5. Place a sheet of greased baking paper or aluminum foil on the wood pellet smoker grill and place the salmon on it, skin side down. Place a few lemon slices on top.

 **INTOLERANCES**

Gluten-Free
Egg-Free
Lactose-Free

6. Put the casserole dish on the fire so that the sawdust begins to smoke. Close it tightly.
7. Leave to smoke for 15 to 20 minutes over medium heat. Check if the salmon is sufficiently smoked. The flesh of the salmon should still be bright orange inside but should come off. If this is not yet the case, continue smoking.
8. Take the salmon out of the casserole dish, place it on a dish, cover with aluminum foil and let stand for 15 min.
9. Just before serving, sprinkle the salmon with a few drops of lemon juice, collected in the casserole dish. Serve with wild rice.

SHOPPING LIST

- 1 lemon
- 2 sprigs of dried fennel (optional)
- 2 tbsp sawdust (preferably untreated beech)
- 2 tbsp fish spices (choice of mixture)
- 500g salmon fillets with skin

3

10 MINUTES

20 MINUTES

Smoked Salmon with Cucumber

 NUTRITION

Calories: 180, Fat: 13g

Cholesterol: 12mg

Carbs: 5g

Protein: 11g

 INTOLERANCES

Gluten-Free

Egg-Free

Lactose-Free

SHOPPING LIST

- 1 long cucumber
- 1 tablespoon lemon juice
- 1 teaspoon finely chopped dill
- 100g of sour cream
- 12 slices of smoked salmon

DIRECTIONS

1. Peel the cucumber and cut it in half lengthwise. Scrape the seeds out with a teaspoon and cut the halves into thin bows.
2. Mix them in a bowl with 1 teaspoon of salt. Let stand for 10 minutes.
3. Squeeze the excess moisture out of the cucumber and add the lemon juice and the dill.
4. Stir the sour cream with a lot of freshly ground black pepper.
5. Place the salmon on four plates and divide the cucumber and sour cream over it.
6. Season with some freshly ground black pepper. Serve.

15 MINUTES

15 MINUTES

4

Club Sandwich with Smoked Salmon

 NUTRITION

Calories: 350, Fat: 25g
Carbs: 20g, Protein: 18g

 INTOLERANCES

Egg-Free
Lactose-Free

 **SHOPPING LIST**

- 6 slices of whole meal bread
- 50-75 g tapenade from dried tomatoes
- 1/4 cucumber, in thin slices
- 30g of arugula
- 200g warm smoked salmon steaks, in pieces
- lemon juice

 DIRECTIONS

1. Toast the whole meal bread slices in a wood pellet smoker grill pan or in the toaster.
2. Brush the slices with the tapenade. Divide the cucumber slices, the arugula and the salmon pieces over 4 slices.
3. Sprinkle some lemon juice over it and generously grind black pepper on top.
4. Place the slices on top of each other on two plates and cover the sandwiches with the last slices with the tapenade down.
5. Cut the club sandwiches diagonally and, if necessary, fix the halves with skewers.

10 MINUTES | **10 MINUTES** | **2**

Yellow Pea Soup with Smoked Tofu

 NUTRITION

Calories: 110, Carbs: 20g
Protein: 9g

 INTOLERANCES

Gluten-Free
Egg-Free
Lactose-Free

 **SHOPPING LIST**

- 1 onion
- 1 clove of garlic
- 3 tbsp. oil
- 300g yellow peeled peas
- 1 tsp vegetable soup paste, (health food store)
- 1 vegetable stock
- 450g Hokkaido pumpkin
- 150g organic potatoes
- 100g carrots
- 1 tsp lemon juice
- 200g smoked tofu
- 1 bunch of slender spring onions
- 5 stems lovage
- 1/12bunch of flat-leaf parsley

 DIRECTIONS

1. Finely dice the onion, press the garlic through the press and sauté both in hot oil.
2. Add the peas and vegetable paste, fill up with the stock, bring to the boil and cover and cook over a low heat for 25-30 minutes.
3. Cut the pumpkin into 1 1/2 cm thick slices, carefully scrape out the seeds, cut the pumpkin into cubes about 1 1/2 cm in size, peel the potatoes and cut into 1 1/2 cm cubes.
4. Peel and dice the carrots. Add the pumpkin, potatoes and carrots to the peas after 25-30 minutes and cook covered for another 15 minutes.
5. Put 1/3 of the soup in a tall mixing beaker, puree finely with a cutting stick and put back in the soup. Season heartily with salt, pepper and lemon juice.
6. First cut the tofu into fine slices, then into triangles. Clean the spring onions and cut them into fine rings.
7. Pluck lovage and parsley leaves from the stems, chop finely and add to the soup together with the tofu and spring onions, heat for another 3-4 minutes.

6

20 MINUTES

1 HR 20 MINUTES

Nut Mix on the Grill

 NUTRITION

Calories: 65, Protein: 23g
Carbs: 4g, Fat: 52g

INTOLERANCES

Gluten-Free
Egg-Free
Lactose-Free

 DIRECTIONS

1. Preheat the grill to 250°F with closed lid.
2. In a bowl combine the ingredients and place the nuts on a baking tray lined with parchment paper.
3. Place the try on the grill. Cook 20 minutes.
4. Serve and enjoy!

SHOPPING LIST

- 3 cups Mixed Nuts, salted - 1 tsp. Thyme, dried
- 1 ½ tbsp. brown sugar, packed - 1 tbsp. Olive oil
- 1/4 tsp. of Mustard powder - 1/4 tsp. Cayenne pepper

5 MINUTES

20 MINUTES

8

Bacon BBQ Bites

NUTRITION

Calories: 300, Fat: 35g
Carbs: 5g, Protein: 26g

INTOLERANCES

Gluten-Free

Egg-Free

Lactose-Free

DIRECTIONS

1. Take an aluminum foil and then fold in half. Once you do that, then turn the edges so that a rim is made. With a fork make small holes on the bottom. In this way, the excess fat will escape and will make the bites crispy.
2. Preheat the grill to 350F with closed lid.
3. In a bowl combine the black pepper, salt, fennel, and sugar. Stir.
4. Place the pork in the seasoning mixture. Toss to coat. Transfer on the foil.
5. Place the foil on the grill. Bake for 25 minutes, or until crispy and bubbly.
6. Serve and enjoy!

🧺 SHOPPING LIST

- 1 tbsp. Fennel, ground
- ½ cup of Brown Sugar
- 1 lb. Slab Bacon, cut into cubes (1 inch)
- 1 tsp. Black pepper
- Salt

5 MINUTES

25 MINUTES

8

Smoked Guacamole

NUTRITION

Calories: 50, Protein: 1g
Carbs: 3g, Fat: 4g

INTOLERANCES

Gluten-Free
Egg-Free
Lactose-Free

SHOPPING LIST

- ¼ cup chopped Cilantro
- 7 Avocados, peeled and seeded
- ¼ cup chopped Onion, red
- ¼ cup chopped tomato
- 3 ears corn
- 1 tsp. of Chile Powder
- 1 tsp. of Cumin
- 2 tbsp. of Lime juice
- 1 tbsp. minced Garlic
- 1 Chile, poblano
- Black pepper and salt to taste

DIRECTIONS

1. Preheat the grill to 180F with closed lid.
2. Smoke the avocado for 10 min.
3. Set the avocados aside and increase the temperature of the girl to high.
4. Once heated grill the corn and chili. Roast for 20 minutes.
5. Cut the corn. Set aside. Place the chili in a bowl. Cover with a plastic wrap and let it sit for about 10 minutes. Peel the chili and dice. Add it to the kernels.
6. In a bowl mash the avocados, leave few chunks. Add the remaining ingredients and mix.
7. Serve right away because it is best eaten fresh.
8. Enjoy!

10 MINUTES

30 MINUTES

8

CHAPTER 11
Casserole Recipes

Baked Green Bean Casserole

12

SHOPPING LIST

- 3 lbs. trimmed green beans
- Kosher salt
- 2 tbsp olive oil
- 2 tbsp unsalted butter
- 1/2 lb. shitake or king trumpet mushrooms, sliced
- 1/4 cup minced shallot
- 1/4 cup rice flour
- 2 cups chicken stock
- 1/2 cup sherry cooking wine
- 1 cup heavy cream
- 1 cup grated parmigiano reggiano
- 1 cup slivered almonds, for topping
- 4 cups canola or vegetable oil
- 8 whole, peeled shallots - 1/2 cup rice flour

DIRECTIONS

1. Set the temperature to High and preheat, lid closed for 15 minutes.
2. Fill a large stockpot 2/3 full of water and bring to a boil over high heat. Prepare a large ice bath. When the water is boiling, add 1 tbsp. of salt.
3. After the water has returned to a rolling boil, add half of the green beans. Cook until al dente, about 2 minutes. Remove with a strainer and place the beans in the ice bath to cool.
4. Remove the green beans from the water and place on paper towels to dry. Repeat with the remaining green beans.

To make the Sauce:

5. Melt the butter and olive oil in a small saucepan over medium heat.
6. Add the shallots and mushrooms and a generous pinch of salt and cook, stirring, until the mushrooms are soft, about 5 minutes.
7. Sprinkle the rice flour over the top and stir to coat the mushrooms and cook off the raw flour taste, about 2 minutes.
8. Add the sherry, stir and reduce, then slowly stir in the stock, allowing to thicken and ensuring there are no lumps, about 3 minutes.

10 MINUTES

50 MINUTES

Corn and Cheese Chile Rellenos

12

DIRECTIONS

1. Put the tomatoes, garlic, onion, and jalapeno in a shallow baking dish and place on the grill grate.
2. Start grill on Smoke with the lid open until the fire is established (4 to 5 minutes).
3. Set the temperature to 450°F and preheat, lid closed, for 10 to 15 minutes.
4. Arrange the New Mexican chilis and the sweet corn on the grate and grill until the chilis are blistered and blackened in spots and the corn is lightly browned, 15 to 20 minutes for the chilis and 10 to 15 minutes for the corn, turning with tongs as needed.
5. Stir the tomato-onion mixture once or twice and remove it from the grill grate when the tomatoes begin to break down. Let all the vegetables cool.
6. Reduce the heat to 350°F if you intend to bake the rellenos right away.
7. Put the cooled tomato mixture in a blender and liquefy.
8. Pour into a saucepan.

30 MINUTES

1 HR 10 MINUTES

SHOPPING LIST

- 2 lbs. Ripe Tomatoes, Chopped
- 4 cloves garlic, chopped
- 1/2 cup sweet onion, chopped
- 1 jalapeno, stemmed, seeded, and chopped
- 8 large Green New Mexican Or Poblano Chiles
- 3 ears sweet corn, husked
- 1/2 tsp. Dry Oregano, Mexican, Crumbled
- 1 tsp. Ground cumin
- 1 tsp. Mild chili powder
- 1/8 tsp. Ground Cinnamon
- Salt and Freshly Ground Pepper
- 3 cups Grated Monterey Jack
- 1/2 cup Mexican Crema
- 1 cup queso fresco, crumbled
- Fresh Cilantro Leaves

Mashed Potatoes

 NUTRITION

Calories: 230, Fat: 2g
Carbs: 45g, Protein: 9g

 INTOLERANCES

Gluten-Free
Egg-Free

5 MINUTES

 **SHOPPING LIST**

- 5 lbs. Yukon gold potatoes, large dice
- 1/2 sticks butter, softened
- 1/2 cup cream, room temperature
- Kosher salt, to taste
- White pepper, to taste

DIRECTIONS

1. When ready to cook, set temperature to 300°F and preheat, lid closed for 15 minutes
2. Peel and dice potatoes into 1/2" cubes.
3. Place the potatoes in a foil tin and cover. Roast in the Traeger until tender (about 40 minutes).
4. In a medium saucepan, combine cream and butter. Cook over medium heat until butter is melted.
5. Mash potatoes using a potato masher. Gradually add in cream and butter mixture, and mix using the masher. Be careful not to overwork, or the potatoes will become gluey.
6. Season with salt and pepper to taste. Enjoy!

40 MINUTES

12

Smoked Pickled Green Beans

NUTRITION

Calories: 24, Fat: 0.1g
Carbs: 6g, Protein: 1g

INTOLERANCES

Gluten-Free
Egg-Free
Lactose-Free

SHOPPING LIST

- 1 lb. green beans, blanched
- 1/2 cup salt
- 1/2 cup sugar
- 1 tbsp red pepper flake
- 2 cups white wine vinegar
- 2 cups ice water

DIRECTIONS

1. Set temperature to 180°F and preheat, lid closed for 15 minutes.
2. Place the blanched green beans on a mesh grill mat and place mat directly on the grill grate.
3. Smoke the green beans for 30-45 minutes until they've picked up the desired amount of smoke. Remove from grill and set aside until the brine is ready.
4. In a medium sized saucepan, bring all remaining ingredients, except ice water, to a boil over medium high heat on the stove.
5. Simmer for 5-10 minutes then remove from heat and steep 20 minutes more. Pour brine over ice water to cool.
6. Once brine has cooled, pour over the green beans and weigh them down with a few plates to ensure they are completely submerged. Let sit 24 hours before use.
7. Enjoy!

20 MINUTES

45 MINUTES

Smoked Apple with Cinnamon

NUTRITION

Calories: 100, Fat: 5g

Protein: 7g

INTOLERANCES

Gluten-Free

Egg-Free

Lactose-Free

SHOPPING LIST

- Golden apples (5-lbs. 2.3-kgs)
- The Rub
- 1/4 cup Lemon juice
- 2 teaspoons Lemon zest
- 1/4 cup Cinnamon
- 3 cups Sugar

DIRECTIONS

1. Preheat the smoker until it reaches the desired temperature prior to smoking.
2. Use apple wood chips for the smoking.
3. Cut the apples into halves then discard the seeds.
4. Combine lemon juice, lemon zest, and sugar then mix well.
5. Rub the apples with the mixture then marinate for about 2 hours or until the sugar mixture becomes liquid.
6. Select "smoke" on the wood pellet smoker and fill the hopper with apple wood chips. Don't forget to soak the wood chips before using.
7. Set the temperature to 225°F (107°C).
8. Arrange the apples on the smoker's rack then smoke for 2 hours or until the apples are tender and golden brown.
9. Once it is done, remove from the smoker and arrange on a serving dish.
10. Serve and enjoy.

15 MINUTES

4 HOURS

10

Sweet Smoked Beans

 NUTRITION

Calories: 140, Fat: 0.3g

Carbs: 35g, Protein: 3g

 INTOLERANCES

Gluten-Free

Egg-Free

Lactose-Free

10

DIRECTIONS

1. Preheat the smoker until it reaches the desired temperature prior to smoking.
2. Use apple wood chips for the smoking.
3. Place the beans in a container then pour water to cover.
4. Soak the navy beans overnight then wash and rinse the beans.
5. Place the beans in a bowl then add chopped onion, brown sugar, red wine vinegar, mustard, garlic powder, and salt into the bowl. Toss to combine.
6. Transfer the beans to a disposable aluminum pan then spread evenly. Pour water over the beans.
7. Fill the hopper with soaked apple wood chips then select "smoke" on the wood pellet smoker. Let the lid open.
8. Set the temperature to 225°F (107°C).
9. Place the aluminum pan on the lowest rack of the wood pellet smoker then smoke for 45 minutes or until the beans are tender.
10. Once it is done, transfer the smoked beans to a serving dish then serve.
11. Enjoy.

 **SHOPPING LIST**

- 1 lbs. Dried navy beans (1-lbs. 0.45-kgs)
- The Spice
- 1 cup Chopped onion
- 3/4 cup Brown sugar
- 1/4 cup Red wine vinegar
- 1/4 cup Molasses
- 1 tablespoon Mustard
- 1 tablespoon Garlic powder
- 1/2 teaspoon Salt
- 3 cups Water

15 MINUTES

45 MINUTES

Smoked Stuffed Avocado with Shredded Chicken

 NUTRITION

Calories: 350, Fat: 20g

Carbs: 18g, Protein: 25g

 INTOLERANCES

Gluten-Free

Egg-Free

10

 **SHOPPING LIST**

- 3 lbs. Ripe avocados

Stuffing:
- 5 cups Pulled chicken
- cups Grated cheese
- 1 ¼ cups Salsa
- 20 Quail eggs

 DIRECTIONS

1. Preheat the smoker until it reaches the desired temperature prior to smoking.
2. Use apple wood chips for the smoking.
3. Cut the ripe avocados into halves then discard the seeds.
4. Preheat a wood pellet smoker then add peach wood pellet to the hopper. Let the lid open.
5. Program the temperature to 375°F (191°C) then close the lid for about 10 minutes.
6. While waiting for the smoke, combine the pulled chicken with salsa and grated cheese then mix well.
7. Top the halved avocado with the chicken and cheese mixture but leave the center.
8. Arrange the stuffed avocados in the smoker then smoke for 25 minutes.
9. After 25 minutes, open the lid.
10. Crack a quail egg then drop in the center of the avocados. Repeat with the remaining avocados and quail eggs.
11. Smoke the avocado again for about 10 minutes or until the eggs are set.
12. Once it is done, take the smoked avocados out from the smoker and arrange on a serving dish.
13. Enjoy right away.

15 MINUTES

45 MINUTES

Smoked Buttery Potatoes

 **NUTRITION**

Calories: 250, Fat: 10g

Carbs: 40g

 INTOLERANCES:

Gluten-Free

Egg-Free

Lactose-Free

15 MINUTES

50 MINUTES

10

 SHOPPING LIST

- 4 lbs. Potatoes
- 1 cup Butter
- 1/4 cup Salt
- 2 ½ tablespoons Black pepper

 DIRECTIONS

1. Preheat the smoker until it reaches the desired temperature prior to smoking.
2. Use cherry wood chips for the smoking.
3. Melt butter over low heat then set aside.
4. Peel the potatoes then cut into slices.
5. Arrange the sliced potato in a disposable aluminum pan then brush with melted butter.
6. Sprinkle salt and black pepper on top then repeat with the remaining potatoes and spices.
7. Preheat a wood pellet smoker then add soaked cherry wood pellet to the hopper. Let the lid open.
8. Program the temperature to 375°F (191°C) then close the lid.
9. Place the pan on the smoker's rack then smoke for 40 minutes.
10. Once it is done, take the pan out from the smoker then serve.
11. Enjoy.

CHAPTER 12

Rub and Salsa
Recipes

Garlic & Salt Pork Rub

 NUTRITION

Calories: 20
Carbs: 5g
Protein: 1g

 INTOLERANCES:

Gluten-Free
Egg-Free
Lactose-Free

5 MINUTES

0 MINUTES

1

SHOPPING LIST

- 8 cloves garlic (minced)
- 1 tbsp. black pepper
- 1 tbsp. paprika
- 1 tbsp. brown sugar
- 1 tbsp. coarse sea salt

 DIRECTIONS

1. Simply place all ingredients into an airtight jar, stir well to combine then close.
2. Use within six months.

Smoked Buffalo Chicken Seasoning Rub

NUTRITION

Calories: 20
Fat: 0.3g
Carbs: 6g
Protein: 1g

INTOLERANCES:

Gluten-Free
Egg-Free
Lactose-Free

5 MINUTES

5 MINUTES

SHOPPING LIST

- 2-3 tbsp. Vegetable oil - 2 tbsp. Onion powder
- 2 tbsp. Cayenne
- pepper
- 2 tsp. Paprika
- 2 garlic cloves, crushed
- 2 tsp. Salt
- 1 to ½ tsp. Black pepper

DIRECTIONS

1. Simply place all ingredients into an airtight jar, stir well to combine then close.
2. Use within six months.

Smoked Thyme Chicken Rub

 **NUTRITION**

Calories: 20
Fat: 1g
Carbs: 6g
Protein: 1g

 **INTOLERANCES:**

Gluten-Free
Egg-Free
Lactose-Free

5 MINUTES

5 MINUTES

1

 SHOPPING LIST

- 1/4 cup olive oil
- 1/4 cup soy marinade
- 2 tbsp. onion powder
- 2 tbsp. cayenne pepper
- 2 tsp. paprika
- 2 garlic cloves, crushed
- 1 to ½ tsp. black pepper
- 1 tsp. dried oregano
- 1 tsp. dried thyme

DIRECTIONS

1. Simply place all ingredients into an airtight jar, stir well to combine then close.
2. Use within six months

Smoked Rub (Turkey BFF)

NUTRITION

Calories: 10
Sugar: 1g
Protein: 2g

INTOLERANCES:

Gluten-Free
Egg-Free
Lactose-Free

5 MINUTES

5 MINUTES

SHOPPING LIST

- 3 tbsp. Onion powder
- 2 tbsp. Paprika
- 1 tbsp. Garlic powder
- 1 tsp. ground Pepper
- 1 tsp. ground Cumin
- 3 tbsp. Vegetable oil

1

DIRECTIONS

1. Simply place all ingredients into an airtight jar, stir well to combine then close.
2. Use within six months.

Smoked Cajun Chicken Rub

NUTRITION

Calories: 5
Carbs: 1g

INTOLERANCES:

Gluten-Free
Egg-Free
Lactose-Free

SHOPPING LIST

- 2 tbsp. Onion powder - 1 tsp. dried Oregano
- 2 tbsp. Cayenne pepper - 2 tsp. Paprika
- 2 tsp. Garlic powder
- 6 tbsp. Louisiana-style hot Marinade
- 2 tsp. Lawry's seasoning salt
- 1 tsp. Black pepper
- 1 tsp. dried Thyme

DIRECTIONS

1. Simply place all ingredients into an airtight jar, stir well to combine then close.
2. Use within six months.

Montreal Steak Rub

5 MINUTES

5 MINUTES

1

NUTRITION

Calories: 19
Fat: 0.5g
Carbs: 3g
Protein: 1g

INTOLERANCES:

Gluten-Free
Egg-Free
Lactose-Free

SHOPPING LIST

- 2 tbsp. salt - 2 tbsp. cracked black pepper
- 2 tbsp. paprika - 1 tbsp. red pepper
- flakes
- 1 tbsp. coriander - 1 tbsp. dill
- 1 tbsp. garlic powder
- 1 tbsp. onion powder

DIRECTIONS

1. Simply place all ingredients into an airtight jar, stir well to combine then close.
2. Use within six months

Sage BBQ Rub

 **NUTRITION**

Calories: 9
Carbs: 1g

 **INTOLERANCES:**

Gluten-Free
Egg-Free
Lactose-Free

5 MINUTES

5 MINUTES

1

 SHOPPING LIST

- 3/4 cup (80g) paprika
- 1/2 cup (100g) sugar
- 1/2 cup (135g) salt
- 1/4 cup (27g) ground black pepper
- 2 tbsp. thyme
- 2 tbsp. dry mustard
- 1 tbsp. cumin
- 1 tbsp. cayenne pepper
- 1 tbsp. sage

 DIRECTIONS

1. Simply place all ingredients into an airtight jar, stir well to combine then close.
2. Use within six months.

Carolina Barbeque Rub

 NUTRITION

Calories: 50
Fat: 0.5g
Carbs: 10g
Protein: 1g

 INTOLERANCES:

Gluten-Free
Egg-Free
Lactose-Free

5 MINUTES

5 MINUTES

 SHOPPING LIST

- 2 tbsp. Salt - 2 tbsp. ground Black pepper
- 2 tbsp. White sugar
- 1/4 cup Paprika
- 2 tbsp. Brown sugar
- 2 tbsp. ground Cumin
- 2 tbsp. Chili powder

1

 DIRECTIONS

1. Simply place all ingredients into an airtight jar, stir well to combine then close.
2. Use within six months.

Memphis Rub

5 MINUTES

5 MINUTES

1

NUTRITION

Calories: 50
Fat: 0.3g
Carbs: 13g
Protein: 1g

INTOLERANCES:

Gluten-Free
Egg-Free
Lactose-Free

SHOPPING LIST

- ½ cup (55g) paprika
- ¼ cup (40g) garlic powder
- ¼ cup (30g) mild chili powder
- 3 tbsp. salt
- 3 tbsp. black pepper
- 2 tbsp. onion powder
- 2 tbsp. celery seeds
- 1 tbsp. brown sugar
- 1 tbsp. dried oregano
- 1 tbsp. dried thyme
- 1 tbsp. cumin
- 2 tsp. dry mustard
- 2 tsp. ground coriander
- 2 tsp. ground allspice

DIRECTIONS

1. Simply place all ingredients into an airtight jar, stir well to combine then close.
2. Use within six months.

BBQ Spice Rub

5 MINUTES

5 MINUTES

1

NUTRITION

Calories: 10
Carbs: 1g
Protein: 1g

INTOLERANCES:

Gluten-Free
Egg-Free
Lactose-Free

SHOPPING LIST

- 1 ½ tsp. onion powder - 2 tbsp. salt - 4 tbsp. paprika
- 1 ½ tsp. garlic
- powder
- 4 tbsp. brown sugar
- 1 tbsp. coarsely ground black pepper
- 2 tsp. mild chili powder
- 1/2 tsp. cayenne pepper (optional)

DIRECTIONS

1. Mix together all the ingredients in a bowl and transfer into an airtight container.
2. Store in a cool dark place. Use as much as required.

Texas Style Brisket Rub

NUTRITION

Calories: 21
Fat: 1g
Carbs: 3g
Protein: 1g

INTOLERANCES:

Gluten-Free
Egg-Free
Lactose-Free

1

5 MINUTES

5 MINUTES

SHOPPING LIST

- 6 tablespoons kosher salt
- 2 tablespoons coarsely ground black pepper
- 4 tablespoons garlic powder
- 10 tablespoons

- paprika
- 6 tablespoons onion powder
- 2 teaspoons mild chili powder
- 1 teaspoon ground coriander
- 4 teaspoons ground

- cumin
- 2 teaspoons dried oregano
- 1 teaspoon garlic powder
- ½ teaspoon cayenne pepper

DIRECTIONS

1. Mix together all the ingredients in a bowl and store in an airtight container.
2. Store in a cool dark place. Use as much as required.

Turkey Wet and Dry Rub

 **NUTRITION**

Calories: 10
Sugar: 1g
Protein: 2g

 INTOLERANCES:

Gluten-Free
Egg-Free
Lactose-Free

5 MINUTES

10 MINUTES

 SHOPPING LIST

- 4 tablespoons onion powder - 4 teaspoons garlic powder
- 2 teaspoons ginger powder - 2 tablespoons paprika
- 4 teaspoons canning salt - 4 teaspoons white pepper powder
- 1 teaspoon sage powder
- ½ cup vegetable oil

 DIRECTIONS

1. Add all the ingredients except oil in a bowl and mix well.
2. Transfer into an airtight container and store.
3. Use as much as required for dry rub.

Kansas City Rib Rub

NUTRITION

Calories: 14
Fat: 0.7g
Carbs: 2g
Protein: 0.1g

INTOLERANCES:

Gluten-Free
Egg-Free
Lactose-Free

5 MINUTES

5 MINUTES

1

SHOPPING LIST

- 1 ¼ teaspoons black pepper - ¼ cup brown sugar
- 1 ¼ teaspoons onion powder - ½ teaspoon cayenne pepper
- 2 tablespoons paprika
- 1 ¼ teaspoons garlic powder
- 1 ¼ teaspoons salt
- 1 ¼ teaspoons chili powder

DIRECTIONS

1. Mix together all the ingredients in a bowl and transfer into an airtight container.
2. Store in a cool dark place. It can last for 6 months. Use as much as required

Chili Wet Rub

NUTRITION

Calories: 10
Sodium: 520mg
Carbs: 2g

INTOLERANCES:

Gluten-Free
Egg-Free
Lactose-Free

5 MINUTES

10 MINUTES

SHOPPING LIST

- ½ cup chili powder
- ¼ cup lemon juice
- ¼ cup sea salt
- 2 tablespoons garlic powder
- 1 teaspoon coarsely ground pepper
- 2 teaspoons cayenne pepper

1

DIRECTIONS

1. Mix together all the ingredients in a bowl and transfer into an airtight container.
2. Store in the refrigerator for up to 2 weeks. Use as much as you please.

Onion Spice Rub

NUTRITION

Calories: 20
Fat: 0.1g
Carbs: 4g
Protein: 1g

INTOLERANCES:

Gluten-Free
Egg-Free
Lactose-Free

5 MINUTES

5 MINUTES

1

SHOPPING LIST

- 1 ½ tsp. onion powder - 2 tbsp. salt
- 4 tbsp. paprika - 1 ½ tsp. garlic powder
- 2 tbsp. brown sugar - 2 tbsp. grounded onion
- 1 tbsp. coarsely ground black pepper
- 2 tsp. mild chili powder
- 1/2 tsp. cayenne pepper (optional)

DIRECTIONS

1. Mix together all the ingredients in a bowl and transfer into an airtight container.
2. Store in a cool dark place. Use as much as required.

Coffee Meat Rub

NUTRITION

Calories: 10
Sodium: 320mg
Carbs: 2g

INTOLERANCES:

Gluten-Free
Egg-Free
Lactose-Free

5 MINUTES

5 MINUTES

1

SHOPPING LIST

- 2 tbsp coffee beans, ground - 2 tbsp black pepper, ground
- 1 ½ tbsp kosher salt

- 1/2 tsp cayenne pepper - 1 tbsp cumin, ground

DIRECTIONS

1. Dry fry the coffee in a roasting pan over medium heat until releases fragrance.
2. Using a container, mix the coffee, black pepper, kosher salt, cayenne pepper and ground cumin.
3. Use the rub on steak before grilling.

Cocoa Rub

5 MINUTES

5 MINUTES

 **NUTRITION**

Calories: 10
Fat: 0.3g
Carbs: 3g
Protein: 1g

 INTOLERANCES:

Gluten-Free
Egg-Free
Lactose-Free

 SHOPPING LIST

- ¼ cup sea salt
- 2 tsp cocoa powder, unsweetened
- 1 tbsp white sugar
- 2 tbsp brown sugar, dark
- 3 tbsp garlic powder
- 1 tbsp onion powder
- 3 tbsp cumin, ground
- 2 tbsp chili powder
- 2 tbsp black pepper, ground

 DIRECTIONS

1. In an airtight container, mix the sea salt, unsweetened cocoa, white sugar, dark brown sugar, garlic powder, onion powder, ground cumin, chili powder and ground black pepper until well-combined.
2. Use 2 to 3 tablespoons on meats before grilling and store the extras covered at room temperature.

Classic Rosemary Dry-Rub

 NUTRITION

Calories: 20g
Fat: 2g
Carbs: 2g

INTOLERANCES:

Gluten-Free
Egg-Free
Lactose-Free

 6

 5 MINUTES

 5 MINUTES

 SHOPPING LIST

- 1 tsp rosemary, dried
- 1 tsp dried minced garlic
- 1 tsp sea salt
- 1 tsp ground black pepper

DIRECTIONS

1. Use a small container, combine the rosemary, dried minced garlic, salt, and ground black pepper.
2. Massage both sides of the meat before cooking or grilling.

Avocado Cream

NUTRITION

Calories: 30
Fat: 1g
Carbs: 8g
Protein: 3g

INTOLERANCES:

Gluten-Free
Egg-Free
Lactose-Free

5 MINUTES

5 MINUTES

8

SHOPPING LIST

- 2 avocados
- 1 onion
- 1 jalapeño
- ¼ cup parsley leaves
- 1 garlic clove
- ¼ cup wine (better red)
- 1 tablespoon lime juice

DIRECTIONS

1. Put all the ingredients in a blender and mix until homogeneous.
2. Pour in a bowl and serve.

Ginger Dipping Sauce

 NUTRITION

Calories: 30
Fat: 1g
Carbs: 8g
Protein: 3g

 INTOLERANCES:

Gluten-Free
Egg-Free
Lactose-Free

10 MINUTES

30 MINUTES

4

SHOPPING LIST

- 2 tablespoons scallions
- 6 tablespoons ponzu sauce
- 2 teaspoons ginger
- 1 tsp sesame oil
- ¼ tsp salt"

 DIRECTIONS

1. Put all the ingredients in a blender and mix until homogeneous.
2. Pour in a bowl and serve.

Italian Pesto

 NUTRITION

Calories: 25
Fat: 2g
Carbs: 10g
Protein: 5g

 INTOLERANCES:

Gluten-Free
Egg-Free

10 MINUTES

30 MINUTES

4

 SHOPPING LIST

- 2 cloves garlic
- 2 oz. basil leaves
- 2 tablespoon pine nuts
- 1 oz. Parmesan
- ½ cup olive oil

 DIRECTIONS

1. Put all the ingredients in a blender (save a few pine nuts) and mix until all is blended.
2. Add some pieces of pine nuts in the mix
3. Pour in a bowl and serve.

Special Soy Sauce

 NUTRITION

Calories: 30
Fat: 1g
Carbs: 8g
Protein: 3g

INTOLERANCES:

Gluten-Free
Egg-Free
Lactose-Free

10 MINUTES

30 MINUTES

4

SHOPPING LIST

- 1/4 cup of soy sauce
- 1/4 cup of rice vinegar
- 1/4 cup of sugar
- 1/2 cup of scallions
- 1/3 cup cilantro"

 DIRECTIONS

1. Put all the ingredients in a blender and mix until homogeneous.
2. Pour in a bowl and serve.

Mexican Dip

 NUTRITION

Calories: 40
Fat: 5g
Carbs: 40g
Protein: 10g

 INTOLERANCES:

Gluten-Free
Egg-Free

 SHOPPING LIST

- 2 tablespoons of black bean paste
- 2 tablespoons of smooth peanut butter
- 1 tablespoon maple syrup
- 2 tablespoons of extra virgin olive oil

10 MINUTES

30 MINUTES

4

 DIRECTIONS

1. Put all the ingredients in a blender and mix until all is blended.
2. Pour in a bowl and serve.

Chimichurri

 NUTRITION

Calories: 30
Fat: 1g
Carbs: 8g
Protein: 3g

INTOLERANCES:

Gluten-Free
Egg-Free
Lactose-Free

10
MINUTES

30
MINUTES

4

SHOPPING LIST

- 1 cup parsley   flakes
- 2 garlic cloves
- 1 tablespoon of dry oregano
- ¼ cup olive oil
- ¼ cup wine vinegar
- ½ tsp red pepper

 DIRECTIONS

1. Put all the ingredients in a blender and mix until homogeneous.
2. Pour in a bowl and serve.

THANK YOU

CPSIA information can be obtained
at www.ICGtesting.com
Printed in the USA
BVHW011530010321
601386BV00002B/266